# Mildred's Wedding, by Francis Derrick
by Frances Eliza Millett Notley

Copyright © 2019 by HardPress

Address:
HardPress
8345 NW 66TH ST #2561
MIAMI FL 33166-2626
USA
Email: info@hardpress.net

# MILDRED'S WEDDING.

VOL. II.

# MILDRED'S WEDDING.

## A Family History.

BY FRANCIS DERRICK,

AUTHOR OF "THE KIDDLE-A-WINK."

IN THREE VOLUMES.
VOL. II.

"Already full of years and heaviness,
I turn to former thoughts of young desires."
MICHAEL ANGELO.

LONDON:
FREDERICK WARNE AND CO.
BEDFORD STREET, COVENT GARDEN.
1865.

LONDON:
CLAYTON AND CO., TEMPLE PRINTING WORKS,
BOUVERIE STREET, E.C.

# MILDRED'S WEDDING.

## CHAPTER I.

PRUDENCE was right when she said I looked at her wishfully. I was thinking of my mother, who had come into my life like a dream, and seemed now like a dream departed.

"Prudence," said I, faintly, "you have told me nothing about mamma."

"I would rather not, Miss Esther; she suited your papa, and that's enough. He was not bound to marry to please an old servant, though she may love him like a mother."

Thinking of the man Paul and my mother's declaration, the horror of which had been the last blow that struck me into fever, I thought it best not to press Prudence with questions on a point that might lead to dangerous topics. Pondering thus, I abruptly changed the subject.

"Who is it says the ghost of Alicia Tremaine haunts Treval?" I asked, and a sudden throb of my heart, a slight paleness of cheek, accompanied my question.

"Many and many say she does," answered Prudence, "but then they say too that the admiral walks through the Towers of Treganowen, and there are others who declare they've seen the unfortunate lieutenant dashing himself from the window, as if he was bent upon killing his own ghost, so I never heed such tales, Miss Esther. I can only tell you I never saw my poor master, or any other ghost either here or at Treval."

"But suppose *I* had, Prudence, what would you say then?"

"I should say you were light-headed, Miss Esther, or had mistook your shadow for a spirit."

"Prudence, I declare to you I saw at Treval a crouching, groping figure such as you describe, and I was not light-headed, and I had no shadow, for I was nearly in darkness. I was on the roof, not on the outside, but beneath the leads."

"Do you feel well to-night, Miss Esther?" interrupted Prudence, regarding me with a scrutinizing look. "This is just the way you went on when you had the fever. We won't talk any more; you had better go to bed, miss."

I found by my father's manner the next day that Prudence White had repeated to him my imprudent speech. He took me out for a ride, and after a long gallop on the moor he directed our way steadily to the sea.

A glorious sun, set in a sky of deepest sapphire, shone down on us, filling every vein with rejoicing; the ever-flowering gorse, faint with its load of perfume, the bruised thyme, the wild mint and chamomile yielded their fragrance beneath the ringing feet of our horses; the air was clear, and fresh, and pure beyond a citizen's dream, and from every peeping cottage garden, hidden between huge rocks, or resting against some giant mass of granite, there came wafted to our lips the scent of may and lilac, of lily, stock, and roses. I breathed this perfumed atmosphere with intense delight. I felt the beauty of earth aad sky filling my whole being, feeding me with a spiritual bread, that satisfied the hunger and thirst of my soul, while every thought ran freer, and the rich, happy blood of youth dyed my cheeks with brightest rose.

At a sudden turn, where the bridle-road edged the cliff with a sharp danger, my father drew rein and stopped.

"Esther," he said, "such a sight as this should surely chase away all sickly fancies."

Nothing could be more beautiful than the scene before us. Such a vision might have haunted Tasso in his dungeon, bringing joy to his wrung heart, spite of the sharp pang felt as its beauty faded away, and the prison wall loomed out in cruel reality through his dream.

"I stood entranced, so bathed in the charm, so steeped in the fulness of sight, that my being seemed suddenly large enough to hold a very heaven of happiness, and a sea, not of thought, but of *life*, rushed over me wave after wave, unutterable for joy, unspeakable in words.

Before us lay the ocean, sublimely blue, calm, deep, mystic; filled with voices like the rush of angel-wings travelling in their strength, scattering from their pinions whispers of doom—voices whose words are sealed up, not to be interpreted by human tongue, and yet speaking to the soul in a language so dear, that the heart leaps up at the sound, and tears of tenderness spring to the eyes, as the first dash of the ocean spray touches our charmed ears.

What Englishman lives, so untrue to his island, that his heart does not bound at sight of the blue waves, with their curled locks of foam, dashing forward to meet his feet, and beating out a welcome to him in glorious music, as they rush over the golden sands? Then, if the stout Anglo-Saxon loves the sea, what is it to the warm, impulsive Cornish Celt, whose narrow granite ridge of land runs out like a tongue to lap the waves, and wind-beaten, rock-bound, and sea-girt, stands in the midst of the waters smiling in verdure and joy?

Truly to him the sea is a thing of life, his nursing-mother, his playmate, his friend; he lays his hand upon the crest of the waves as the English rider on his horse's mane, and caresses the deep waters, loving them equally whether basking calmly in the summer sky, or lashed to fury by the arms of the north-west wind.

With this mystic love glowing warmly at my heart I looked down upon the scene below. A long slope of matted heath and sea herbage, soft, elastic, and deeply green, had conducted us to the verge of the cliff. There was no beach lying at the foot of this dizzy precipice; like a giant wall, black, perpendicular, terrible, it raised itself against the waves, which laved its base at all times of the tide. Here the huge rocks, polished by the lapping waters, displayed their flashing colours to the sun, and gave back to the transparent depths the purple and rose tints, the changing green and black of their veined masses.

But words fail me when I would tell the colours of the serpentine and the sea on this lovely coast. The dark green of the rocks veined with scarlet throws a rose flush over the water, which, mingling with its vivid green and deep blue shadows, blends all into one glorious, inexpressible hue, changing, flashing, sparkling from beauty to beauty with every varying light. Clear, clear as purest crystal, are these deep, rolling waves, so that bright pebbles, and vivid rocks of serpentine, and dark seaweeds reposing in their stilly depths shine out in calm distinctness far beneath the eye, their glancing lights and massy shadows, so pure in this transparent water, adding an elfin and mysterious charm to the rosy sea. One might deem the abodes of the sea nymphs and the jewelled caves of mermaids are lying there bared to the curious eye, the flashing serpentine, gemmed and streaked with ardent colours, seeming a fitting palace for their habitation.

In gazing down the dizzy precipice, with curious eye long searching, I could trace, where the spray lapped the rock in a long shining roll, the streaks of red like creeping veins of blood meandering through the blackness, and the radiant tints of green, and orange, and crimson that shine out in the polished serpentine; but from above the cliff these bright colours scarcely tinge the funereal black of that sombre wall which, near the cavern of Pigeon Hugo, raises itself against the sweeping roll of the Atlantic, surging in with a ceaseless moan, like the wail of a boundless sorrow crying to the earth.

At Dollah Hugo * the lowly colours of rock and sea are more plainly visible, but enough of beauty was here to keep me silent as I gazed out upon the loveliness of sea and land, clad in their bright garment

\* The Dean of Canterbury, in a late paper in *Good Words*, prefers the cave of Dollah Hugo to the famed *grotta azzurra* at Capri. He also says that the Cornish sea has very little to fear in comparison with the Mediterranean at Amalfi and Capri.

of sunshine, fanned by the western wind, whose whisper is the scent of flowers, and lulled by the music of the waves kissing the sea-girt rock.

In the same silence of this intense joy—which is almost pain in its depth—we turned away, and rode on for a mile before uttering a word. Before such scenes the tongue is tied and powerless; it is the soul that speaks, and this has no human words for its interpreter. In the presence of immortal beauty it recognises its kinship with the eternal, a brotherhood with all truth and loveliness; it feels an aspiration towards joy like the stir of living wings, and with this mingles the pain of loss, the mystery of a heaven forgotten, forfeited, and a pining, a longing that quenches hope in tears.

Past Pradanack Head and Mullion Island we rode on, and still I had made no answer to my father's remark respecting sickly fancies. And I was not sorry, because it was a scene in keeping with my thoughts, when he stopped at a little church standing on high ground, and therefore a conspicuous object even from the bay.

"We have reached Mullion Church, Esther, and there is a tomb here I want you to see. Let me help you to alight."

We fastened our horses by the old Cornish stile, and entered the church. In the chancel my father stopped and showed me this epitaph:—

"THOS. FLAVEL, Vicar of Mullion.
"Died 1682.

"Earth, take thine earth, my sin let Satan havet,
The world my goods, my soul my God who gavet;
For from these four—Earth, Satan, World, and God—
My flesh, my sin, my goods, my soul I had."

"What a pity this good man is not living now, Esther!" said my father, with a glance at me.

"Why?" I asked, surprised at the tone in which he spoke.

"Because he was the celebrated ghost-layer of the West. Not a haunted house in Cornwall which he did not visit and free from its troubled guest; not a single spectre-haunted man or woman for whom he did not pray, and on whom he did not lay the calm holy hands which drove the evil spirit away. Now are you sorry that he is dead, Esther?"

As my father uttered these words I saw that our long ride through the loveliest scenes of the West, and this visit to the grave of the ghost-layer, were preconcerted things.

"Prudence has told you," I said, softly. "But I do not think the good Thomas Flavel, or any other exorciser, could lay *my* ghost to rest. I saw it, and I was greatly afraid; but what is most strange is that I long to see it again, and I feel I should not be afraid."

"Esther," said my father with sorrowful

seriousness, "you are mistaken, you saw nothing; you were even then ill, and had strange images in your brain. Remember that three days afterwards you were struck with fever, and it grieves me to see you retain in health the delusions of sickness. I brought you to this tomb that you might recognise the folly and superstition of an age that induced this good man to believe himself a ghost-layer. We know now this was an illusion of his, but think how his faith in ghosts must have strengthened the terrors of his neighbours, and how many spectres his very presence in a village must have invoked. All illusions are mischievous; throw off yours, Esther, unless you would grieve me."

"One question," said I, a little tremblingly, "and then I will answer you. Was I *mad* during my illness?"

My father paused, much troubled.

"Esther," he said, taking my hand,

"both Dr. Spencer and I foresaw this question of yours, and he advised me to answer it candidly. Still you have asked a harder thing than you suppose, because I cannot reply by either 'yes' or 'no.' During the height of fever you were delirious, but on your recovery, or apparent recovery, you were certainly in possession of all your faculties, memory alone excepted. All your past life was swept away from you, and you recollected only the occurrences that had chanced since your illness,[*] just as since your real recovery you have forgotten all that happened during sickness, and your old life has returned to you, leaving that time a blank. Yet how can we call this blank madness when it showed no loss of sense? On the contrary, faculties were developed in you during this period which either you do not possess at all, or which

[*] Similar cases are mentioned by Dr. Abercrombie in his work on the intellectual powers.

else lie now strangely dormant. Your personality seemed changed in some mysterious way; all this dreamy listless indolence which is your characteristic was changed for an intense vitality and power; accomplishments—not yours, alas! now—darted then easily from your lips and fingers. Dr. Spencer begged me to induce your mind to inquire into its state during this period. Can you remember nothing of all this?"

"Nothing," said I, with a weariness which was but a longing for the old power.

My father looked at me sorrowfully.

"I believe you," he said, "strange as it appears; and all the gifts which enchanted us have left you now your true health is returned, and nothing remains save this one sad delusion of ghosts. I wish this would quit you, Esther, and some of your pretty accomplishments come back in its place. One would think you had two individualities, and that during your illness you showed us your real self—a playful, laughing, singing Esther—which you keep hidden away, and never allow to peep forth now."

My father's tone was a jesting one, but the expression of his eyes as he gazed at me was earnest and inquiring. Beneath his look my nerves thrilled painfully, and thoughts came crowding into my brain heavy with the old fancies I had had at Treval, of a strange duality within me. I tried to shake them off.

"How could I have laughed and sung," I said, "when I was so ill? I remember how weak I was when I woke up at Treganowen."

"For a long time you were quite well and strong at Treval," said my father, "but then you had a return of fever, and it was during this we brought you home, as we saw symptoms of the old, quiet, sad Esther coming back in her normal state of ghost-seeing and dreaminess. Now shall I apostrophize the spirit of the old ghost-layer here, and entreat him to exorcise your spectre, and bring you in its stead the laughter and song that enchanted us?"

My father stretched out his arm playfully towards the quaint epitaph of Thos. Flavel as he spoke, but I laid my hand on his and stopped him.

"Papa," I said, and I felt my voice falter, "you say the shape the new, the strange Esther took at Treval during this illness, this blank of mine, 'enchanted *us*.' Whom do you mean by 'us?' Was mamma pleased? did she like me then?"

My father turned from the tomb of the ghost-layer, and hid his face from me as he answered—

"Even your mother, my dear, cherished you a little then."

"And—and was there any one else?" I asked in a whisper that thrilled through the old chancel like the moan of a spirit in pain.

My father faced me suddenly with a keen searching glance.

"Do you really remember nothing, Esther?" he said.

"Nothing, nothing," I answered in a hopeless tone. I said this, and it was true, and yet not true, for deep down in my heart I felt a strange consciousness of some great love that had wrapped me about in an infinite tenderness, some love I had lost now, and was searching for blindly and in vain.

"Then if you remember nothing, Esther," said my father kindly, "do you not see that if there were others you would not know them—would not recognise even their names?"

"Miss Mildred will not let you tell," said I, with some slight passion in my voice.

My father turned deadly pale, and with hasty, echoing tread strode down the chancel without a word. In the porch he waited for me, and lifted me on my horse.

"Never say that again, Esther," he said, quietly, as he placed the bridle in my hand.

I did not answer, for my heart was full, and my brain felt irritated and oppressed as thought groped dimly through it, seeking a light wherewith to examine this importunate sense of being loved and lost which beat at the portal of my closed memory. In passing through the churchyard a gravestone met my eye, on which I read the words—

"STEPHEN BEDILLA.
Aged 55 years."

The dead man was nothing to me, and the date of his death was long ago, before I was born, yet I repeated his name to myself like one in a dream, saying many times, "Stephen, Stephen."

"Papa, what does the word Stephen mean?"

I pointed with my riding-whip to the stone, which stood almost in our path.

"It means a garland or crown," said my father, riding on abruptly before me.

I thought of the wreath of dead leaves which I had superstitiously locked away, and my lips echoed the words, "A garland—my garland." Then with a sudden vivid blush I sank into a silent reverie. Whose love was this—for love it surely was—that had awoke me from this dead sleep of my chilled existence to a happy life, bringing gifts to my indolent and fitful nature which my dulled mind could not recal now? Was it his? My young heart fluttered at the thought, and the ring of my horse's feet danced in my ears to the words, " Stephen, a garland, a crown of joy."

Alas! when that wreath touched my temples I found it a crown of thorns, twined with sharp suffering and bitter sorrow.

## CHAPTER II.

I was a dull companion to my father that day in our long ride home. In vain he called to me cheerfully to look at the great peak of rocks lying piled up in fantastic pinnacles and towers, and hence called the cathedral.* I looked, but I scarcely saw; neither could I be charmed by the glistening bay of Polurrian, or by ancient Gunwalloe, with its hoar church, stricken by time, and detached belfry, lonely by the sea shore, ringing out its bells to the wild sea.

I was glad when the weary miles brought us into the granite country again, for I loved its barrenness better than the fertile serpentine, though the lovely white

* Near Mullion Cove.

heath,\* which grows only on this stratum, lingered tenderly in my hand as its best remembrance.

As we neared the gates of Treganowen I grew nervous, greatly longing to speak before their gloomy portals swallowed me up. Instinctively I knew my father yearned for a word from me to assure him that these lovely views of heathy earth and open sky had cleared my morbid fancies, and the tomb of the ghost-layer had shamed my superstition; but I could say neither.

"Papa," I cried, forcing my tone to be gay, "you should have dipped me in the well of St. Cuthbert† when I was an infant, to preserve me from the machinations of the Evil One. Nothing else, I fear, would save me from being haunted."

\* The Erica vagans, known by the name of the Cornish heath.

† The holy well here named lies in a cavern by the sea between Penhale Point and Kelsey Head; it is approached by a beach of silvery sand.

"There are many other wells, Esther," said my father; "suppose you try the well of knowledge! You were too wild, too free at Treval. I must begin your education now in earnest, and undo this mischief if I can. I have sent to London for some books purposely for you."

"I wish Prudence had not told you," I answered wearily, "for I feel sure books will not take from me my memory of what is a fact, and not a fancy."

"Prudence's avowal," observed my father, "only gave me the sorrowful assurance that one illusion of fever remains fixed in your mind, for the fact itself—as you erroneously call it — I heard you constantly refer to during your illness, both here and at Clifton."

"And at Treval," I asked eagerly, "where I got so much stronger and better, and where you say I had no delirium—did I speak of it there?"

"Never once," answered my father, emphatically — "at least not to me and Admonitia, and your attendants assure me you never spoke of it to them; the illusion seemed quite vanished. I never saw your mind in a more healthy state; you never talked of this ghost-woman then, Esther, and of course we did not broach the subject: we avoided raising the idea of her again in your brain; and to show your fearlessness, you visited the roof often, both with me and alone. During all your convalescence, until your second attack, I only remarked one eccentricity—you always climbed the great cedar on the lawn every evening to see the sun set."

A sudden pallor overspread my face at his words, and quivering before my eyes the shadow of the blank wall passed in all its ghastly woe.

"It is a pity," said I, glancing with a trembling look at my father, "that my strange relapse should have taken from me all recollection of my stay at Treval."

"It *is* a pity indeed," he answered, in a tone of such deep sorrow that I was startled. "Heaven alone knows what pain might be spared you and me, my child, if on restoration to health you had awoke with a full consciousness of that period; but the time\* is lost to you, and with it———" Here he stopped abruptly, and then by an evident

---

\* Dr. Abercrombie, in his work on the intellectual powers, enumerates, in cases where the brain has been affected, many instances of a total loss of the impression of time with all its attendant circumstances. Speaking of that mysterious disease, somnolency, he mentions a case where a young lady, on recovering from her first attack, was found to have lost every kind of acquired knowledge, and her education had to be recommenced; but on a second attack, with subsequent recovery, she was restored to all the knowledge she possessed before her malady, but she had not the least recollection of anything that had occurred, or any information or accomplishment acquired, during the interval of health between the two attacks—this time, with all its thoughts, its acts, its daily drama of life, was entirely lost to her. I quote this case as one equivalent to Esther's.

effort continued: "I mean in that case I should not now have the pain of combating your singular illusion of having met the spirit-figure of a woman on the roof at Treval."

I sighed deeply, but I refrained from answering. I felt this one memory would ever appear in opposite forms to my father and myself—to him as a spectre of my brain, a phantom raised by disease; to me a tangible shape, which I regarded by some mysterious means in two lights—that is, in the full light of memory with all the attendant horrors that accompanied my creeping journey over the roof, and in a pale glimmer, too faint for memory, too impalpable to be seized by thought, in which I faced the shape, and regarded it without fear or vestige of horror. This singular feeling, this pale sheen of memory, was so subtle, so lightly poised upon my brain, that it eluded my grasp; if by cunning steps of thought I approached it, I found it gone, flown like a swift, or if by force of will I touched it, lo! it died instantly like a gossamer midge in a rough boy's hand. Seeing, then, the impossibility of clothing in words this shadowy, ever-fleeing light, in which the spirit-woman came to me in curious familiar shape, and shrinking from her other form of ghastly horror, I resolved to be silent, and abruptly changed the subject.

"Papa," I said, laying my hand a moment on his arm, "you are not angry at the tale Prudence told me?"

There was an instant and painful emotion visible on my father's face, and he steadied his lips with an effort as he spoke.

"No, my dear. I wished her to say something to you, that, erroneous and unformed as her tale may be, it might yet prepare you for the history I have promised one day to tell you."

My father's hand was on the gate opening to the avenue; I laid mine on his bridle.

"One word more," I said, hurriedly. "I cannot speak in-doors—it kills me. Is mamma coming back, or does she hate me too much to live where I am?"

I did not expect to see such anguish quiver on his face as stood there when he turned it towards me.

"Esther," he said, "your mother will not come back to Treganowen, but I shall go sometimes to see her, and will take you with me whenever you like. I cannot believe she hates you; you do not know her, and you judge wrongly. But never question me about your mother; remember she is also my wife, and perhaps, when you are only seeking to relieve your own pain, you may be cruelly adding to mine. Let us go in—the sun is sinking."

"One thing more, papa; only one, I entreat you. Who is Paul, and what has my mother got to do with him?"

My father looked at me with unfeigned astonishment.

"Paul! what Paul?" he said. Then he put his hand tenderly on my shoulder, as though some sorrowful thought concerning me had struck him.

"My poor Esther," he said, "fling away these delusions of your illness. Neither your mother nor I ever heard of any one called Paul, nor did you, except in your dreams of fever."

I passed through the gate silently, which he held open for me. I remembered I had in my haste half broken the promise made to my mother, and his answer came to me like a relief.

## CHAPTER III.

The books of which my father had spoken arrived. I was a hungry reader, and had they been the veriest garbage of the sentimental school, then at the height of its power, I should still have devoured them. The avidity, then, with which I flung myself on this mental food, on finding it exactly suited to my peculiar idiosyncrasy, can be well imagined. With a beating heart, with flushed cheeks and hot hands, I turned over the pages, devouring the words that told how illness dims the brain, and how before the wearied sight spectres rose and vanished, voices muttered in the vexed ear, and visions came and departed. Still, throughout the whole range of facts placed methodically before my understanding, I observed the patients themselves, if sane, were rarely deceived; their illusion appeared to them an illusion, and they grappled with and conquered it, or else indifferently watched the fleeting apparitions, half-amused by their fantastic wonders. In no instance was there any analogy to my own case. I read here no history of children lonely and spell-bound, who watched through long months for one woful shadow coming and going in dreary monotony against a blank wall. The shadows here were traced back to some indistinct memory, or forgotten tale, or half-remembered dream, or other causes named as ghost-raising; but to none of these could I ascribe that spectre face, and the groping and terrible figure on the roof with which I had so suddenly identified it. The result was that my belief in the *reality* of what I had seen became strengthened, and a determination grew out of my studies which I will name at the right time and in the right place.

None the less did my interest in reading continue, and, above all, I dwelt with throbbing emotion on those narratives which spoke of preternatural hates and loves arising from disease. A bone more or less depressed, a pressure like a feather's weight upon the brain, and lo! we were loving and gentle, or hateful and furious. Wandering in a maze of thought, I began to see dimly how blind all human judgment was, and, pondering on my mother's hatred for me, and mine for Miss Mildred, pity grew up in my heart for both, as Faith with calm hand led me through that labyrinth of mystery which surrounds our double being of mind and matter. Yearning towards the light, led by this new-born pity, a straggling beam of God's infinite love and mercy reached me, and as one spark from the divine rays brightened my darkness, I bowed my head upon my hands, weeping and prayerful. From that day forward the shrinking antipathy I bore to Miss Mildred changed its character, and the sullen resentment against my mother which burned slowly at my heart died away in remorse and compassion.

Thus far my reading did me good, but no further. My dangerous imagination was inflamed with excitement, and my nerves were thrilled with an unhealthy quiver, as I read of trances in which the spirit seemed to leave the body for awhile, returning from distant worlds heavy with unlawful knowledge which the faltering tongue could never impart. In vain for me the cold fingers of science uncovered the mystery, and held the delusion up to the light bared of its mystic folds, discovering its true shape to be disease or madness. The unspiritual explanation given in calm, chilly words made no impression on a mind like mine. For me the mysterious veil rested still upon these strange facts, and I believed and trembled.

Again I read of men and women with sane eyes beholding visions which they wrestled with bravely, knowing them to be the creations of an ill-conditioned physical state. Here was the story of a lady* looking from her window watching a coach driving up to her door, and as it draws nearer the shrinking watcher sees within a crowd of ghastly skeletons. It stops, and one by one these grisly visitors descend and lay a bony hand upon the bell, but there is no sound when they ring, no servant obeys the ghostly summons. Silently the fleshless things glide away, and the sick lady watching knows her dread disease has laid that day a ghastlier hand upon her brain, and her fight now is for reason as well as life.

\* Related by Sir David Brewster in his work on *Natural Magic*.

Nobly she bears the battle; and when at evening, as she sits before a mirror, the face of her dead sister looks over her shoulder and meets her in the glass, she does not shrink; she recognises the phantom of an unsound mind, and, unflinching, gives it back look for look, till healthy thought, conquering the sick imagination, banishes the hideous shadow. I read, I mused, but was not yet convinced. There is a reality in some sights which the arguments of science cannot explain away. My pile of books, with all their learning, could not shake down that pale figure on the roof from its place in my memory, or change one flutter of its garment into the " baseless fabric of a vision."

I set aside these works to study a little book that spoke of strange gifts bestowed in sleep and snatched away on waking. In this quickening slumber the faculties were unchained, and revelled, joyous, in unknown powers. Numbed, perchance, by want and ignorance was the waking brain, but, wrapped in sleep, the soul broke loose from chance and time, and all the chains of circumstance, to clutch with free and happy clasp its gifts divine of poesy and song. Then, flying with glad wings from gift to gift, thought became will, and instant with the will sprang forth the deed, the voice broke into melody perfect and pure—for when thought, and will, and power are perfect, the creations born of these must be perfect too—the hand obeyed the spirit, and glanced over the keys with fingers music's own; the stammering tongue, unskilled in speech, and rude with rustic thought, burst from its trammels, and revelled, glorious, over a field of language golden with images of heaven, silver with the sheen of earth; and all the innate, inborn, and struggling genius, stifled long in sleep and clay, sprang with a glad leap into life and into action. The power to create, to do, is the test of genius; by their works shall we know them who wear its unseen crown.

As I hung breathless over these histories of a fettered power set free, my heart beat painfully, and a sick longing like the faintness of death seized my spirit. I too had this stir within me as of unknown wings—I too felt that I was not living my *whole* life—that something was concealed, hid away from me by unseen hands, and I wept for very bitterness, and beat the darkness blindly as I sought to escape from the mysterious shackles that held my soul closely enchained.

Alas! I was like a prisoner striking useless blows on the walls of his dungeon, to whose senses only returns the dreary echo of his own vain efforts to be free.

In sleep, then, these sadder prisoners of fate and circumstance have been set free, and the rapt ears of listeners have hung as in a charm on eloquence poured forth in silvery floods, or raging with all the might and liberty of battle.

And, O heavens! when this rich sleep was over, and the poor crushed brain held down by ignorance, and coarser toil came back with heavy fall to its dead, dull day, learned doctors come together called this awakening!

Sickness, was it? Yes; then let it be sickness, if they would; but it was a sickness that had a score of sound healths in it, and a life running through its veins that surely sprang from some brighter world than this.

"And here is Miss Admonitia," said I wearily, "driving up the avenue in her old landau, with her old ideas that, because I am a child in years, she who has helped to make me a weird old woman must treat me like a child still. I will not question her;

she will tell me nothing, and I shall grope on blindly among these mysteries till I die or go mad; or, worse still, she will give me a half-confidence, a new secret to keep, and will not see that I am weary, weary, weary."

## CHAPTER IV.

LISTLESSLY I put away my book, and with languid footfall descended the great staircase, one part of my thoughts childishly counting the steps, or wondering if the painted eyes of shepherdess and warrior portraits had not now and then some evil spirit looking out of them, while the other part of my thoughts soared away into yearnings unutterable for pain and longing, where sharp thorns pierced my feet as I travelled on, and my outstretched hands seeking passionately beat the wall, and a voiceless cry upon my lips for peace died away in darkness.

Unconsciously my feet brought me to Miss Admonitia's side, and my small hand lay languidly in hers, ere I awoke and looked upon her face. Then I started, for she was changed—changed, I mean, from that time before the blank when I was afraid of her, and her brow had always worn a frown. Now she was paler, sadder, thinner, but there was a something shining in her eyes for me never there before—a something I could only call *love*, and wonder at with a sort of sick fear. Yes, fear, because the love was for that unknown Esther for whom even now I was blindly seeking—that Esther of the blank time, nursed at Treval during the bleak winter days, warmer to me than summer sunshine.

And for me, the grey, pale Esther, standing by her side, the love died out of her eyes in a cloud of chill disappointment as she relinquished my hand and said coldly—

" Well, Esther, child, how are you ? "

" I am well," I answered in my old

dreamy voice. Then I started, and, in spite of my efforts, a something, I know not what, broke its chains within me, and, bursting its bonds like a thread, flung me wildly at Miss Admonitia's feet. Yet I spoke calmly, in a quiet voice, a low, thrilling whisper unnatural to my own ears. "Did I say well? No, Miss Admonitia—I am going mad. Sit still and hear me; I shall die now if you do not let me speak. I am not the poor, tamed, frightened child brought up in loneliness; I am the wild spirit broken loose whom you have nursed in haggard fear—you and Miss Mildred—and fed on mysteries and silent hate. Well, I return it. Hear me—I hate you both. I will not be held in bondage by you. I do not care what compact you have made with my father; I renounce it. I break your bonds asunder. I will *not* be driven mad!"

With dry and fiery eyes I looked up into

her face, while my parched lips refused to obey my will, and ceased to speak, as, quivering and pale, they remained parted in trembling eagerness.

"Poor, silly, ignorant child!" said Miss Admonitia, gazing down on me with the old dusky red flushing hot over her cheeks. "I will try not to be angry at your blind ingratitude and injustice. I will not ruin you by letting you free."

"Leave me alone!" said I, tearing at her hands as she strove to hold me. "Let me go! I shall kill you!"

She released me and flung me from her heavily, as we fling a creature we dislike, but, save that her very brow was dark now with that angry flush, she showed no sign of passion.

"Ah! fling me off like that for ever!" said I in a deep, sulky tone, "and let me tell my father that we are free!"

Miss Admonitia tightened her arms

across her chest, and held herself down as we hold some wild animal.

"My God!" she murmured, "have we not suffered enough, I and my sisters, from this race?—and must we nurse a viper of their blood to sting us? Esther"—and she writhed with the intensity of her disgust towards me—"if it depended on me, I would willingly let you leave us for ever; you might go away, a beggar, and perish beneath a hedge. But if *I* am unmerciful, it is Mildred who will fast and pray— Mildred who will watch and weep for my sin. There—go; for her sake I forgive you. God help me! what have I not forgiven you and yours for her sake!"

Her stateliness gave way, her face died back to its old paleness, and she sank into a chair, with a perceptible shiver running through her frame. I stood before her unmoved, with my old dreaminess and apathy creeping back chilly upon my brain.

"Well," said I wearily, "then I am in bondage still. Secrets weighing down upon me on every side. A shut door between my father and me—a barrier of dislike growing like a wall, dividing me from my mother, and you and Miss Mildred still pitiless save for yourselves."

"Stop!" said Miss Admonitia huskily; "you do not know what you are saying. Pity! A tender pity like an angel's has been round you ever since you were born. Speak of your other grief—what is it?—secrets?"

"Yes," said I coldly. My passion was fast fading away, and I was ceasing to care how it ended, or what happened.

"Well, tell me what secrets most torment you, and I will do away with them if I can."

And now, instead of demanding what most interested me, instead of seeking for any clue to my labyrinths, I looked at her with my thoughts afar off, dwelling on an old melody which seemed to be floating near me now without my being able to seize it; and I answered stupidly—

"Why have you and Miss Mildred refused to let me learn music?"

"Does that annoy you?" said Miss Admonitia. "Mildred thought it would make you unhappy. We have seen great sorrow spring from these vain accomplishments. But she has changed lately; she wishes now herself that you should learn music."

"Why?" said I, quickly.

"Because—because we know you wish it. Have you anything else to ask?"

"Yes. What does my mother hate me for?"

"Esther, why does your father love you? You cannot answer me, neither can I answer you. I only know that your mother will never love any human being that your father loves, hence for your sake he would have hidden his affection; but it was enough for her to suspect it; that sufficed her, and brought upon you her aversion. Be content with your father's love—a love so prized that I have seen a daily death of years crush a heart that lost it."

I was silent, with a great throb of compunction at my own heart.

"Have you anything else to ask, Esther?"

"Yes," said I, turning suddenly towards her with a flash of new energy. "Who is Paul? And if he murdered your sister, why not hunt the villain through the world till he hangs upon the gibbet he deserves?"

Miss Admonitia hid her face in her hands at my bold words, and her figure shrank as if she had received a painful blow. Even when she took her hands away and held one towards me—not to invite my approach, but to wave me off—she still shut her eyes, as we do involuntarily in a spasm of pain.

"I was not sure she heard those mad words of her mother's," she muttered to herself.

She rose hurriedly, as if some feeling were too strong for her, and paced the room; then stopping suddenly behind me, she seized me by the arm and turned my face towards her.

"You meant those words for an insult," she said—"an insinuation against Mildred? Answer."

"Perhaps I did," I replied, doggedly.

A flush came hotly over her face, her eyes flashed fire.

"I don't see why I should show you the great mercy," she cried, "of keeping you in blindness. Mildred can be a saint—I cannot. She can bear uncomplaining your father's hatred and your ingratitude—I cannot. Or if I can bear them for myself, I cannot for her. I will answer your first question. *Paul is your mother's only brother!*

Now find out for yourself why we do not hunt him through the world to the gallows."

She released me with a gesture of contempt, and as her hot clasp abandoned my arm I reeled forward and caught her by the gown. Every sudden emotion had a singular effect upon me. My whole brain seemed shaken, and for a moment I always felt stunned, the next I became conscious of some indefinable change in myself, some instantaneous transition of mood and feeling. It was the case now. As her dreadful words pierced me through and through with anguish, my hardness, my apathy, my dull hate vanished, and hiding my face in the folds of her robe, and clinging to her with clasping passionate fingers I burst into bitter tears.

"Oh, Miss Admonitia!" I sobbed, "I deserved that you should tell me this. I understand now, it is mercy to me, mercy to my father, that holds you and your sister back. You let the murderer go free out of pity to his wretched kin."

I wrung my hands, I trembled, I writhed before this new, horrible, and *real* misery. I felt like a worm transfixed by the hook, like a felon shrinking from the burning brand. I clasped Miss Admonitia's knees, and moaned in my pain like some wounded animal.

My mother's brother the murderer of Alicia! A felon's blood in my veins! a man to be tracked down through the world by his fellow-men, a man around whose villanous shadow there curdled a pool of innocent blood, and whose footsteps were marked by crime—he my uncle, my nearest relative!

"O comfort me! comfort me!" I cried. "Say it is not true! Say you said it to punish me!"

Miss Admonitia was greatly moved; she raised me kindly.

"Would to Heaven I could say it was not true, Esther!" she said. "O! would I could live these few minutes over again, then I would spare you this. I am not fit to be trusted with a Treganowen by myself. You are a wayward and terrible child, Esther, but Mildred would have borne all your cruel words meekly, and have paid you back with heaped kindness, and you would have left her hating her, and blind as you always have been. Perhaps I have been cruel in opening your eyes, but you must take your share now in our burden, and help us to spare your father. He does not know such a man exists as Paul Polwhele."

I was mad with misery and pain. I could not reply. My pride of birth, my pride of ancestry, my passionate feeling of honour, my joyful innocence, all lay crushed within me, or started up bleeding to protest against this shame.

"O let me die!" I moaned, "for how can I live, and bear this degradation?"

Miss Admonitia clasped her hands together with a troubled look, but she forbore to answer me. Perhaps she was thinking of Mildred's long suffering and patience under the shame so unjustly laid on her by the hand she most loved.

"Esther," said Miss Admonitia at last, when I had wept till I was exhausted, "rouse yourself! Your father will soon return from his ride, and you must not show him such a face as this."

"You could not—you could not have known," said I, wringing her hand in mine, "who Paul was when you married my mother to my father?"

"No," answered Miss Admonitia, drily; "when Mildred and I recommended Miss Polwhele to your father, it was not likely we could guess her brother was the murderer of Alicia."

"Then you knew she had a brother," I continued, persistently, "and you helped her to keep this fact a secret from my father?"

"Esther, you *force* me to say cruel things," replied Miss Admonitia, in a shrinking tone. "Must I tell you that your mother lied to me, lied to your father, lied to Mildred? Must I tell you that she has lied all her life long, and will continue to lie while her life lasts? There—let us finish this painful conversation. She told us her brother was dead; had we known him to be living she would never have been Mrs. Treganowen. We were not ignorant that he had been a wild scamp, but a thief and a murderer we scarcely thought him. But since he is both, and she has concealed his existence from your unhappy father, it remains for us to consider whether for his sake concealment is not the greatest kindness we can show him. Think it over yourself, and divulge the fact if you judge best, only remember *he* will not spare the murderer of Alicia."

I sat silent, in deep consternation. Miss Admonitia had the advantage, and circumstances were too strong for me. I saw my violence to-day had only added an additional weight to my burden, without clearing away a single cloud from the dark mysteries that tormented my life. Doubtless my face expressed somewhat of the utter prostration of feeling that possessed me, for Miss Admonitia responded to it sorrowfully:—

"Are you the only one, Esther, that has a grief to bear? Until lately you have been spared, and others have suffered for you. And is it altogether my fault if your load is made heavier to-day by your knowledge of a fact which we would fain have kept from you? Your temper wrung it from me—I did not tell it willingly."

I remained silent beneath her reproach, for I knew I deserved it.

"And now," continued Miss Admonitia, "that you have to share this wretched secret with Mildred and myself, display some of her courage, her resignation, and abnegation of self, and for your father's and mother's sake be silent and careful."

"But is it not wrong, is it not wicked, to let this man escape?" I asked, anxiously, as I felt my face blanch at the thought of crimes the unshackled murderer might yet commit.

"*I* think so," answered Miss Admonitia, in a tone of deep dejection, "but Mildred differs from me. The great sorrows of her life give her the right to demand what she will of me. She demands that this man shall live. She demands my secrecy, and I give it, although my conscience tells me that I am acting against duty. Yes, my sad opinion is that at *all costs*—life, fortune, honour, peace—it is our duty to denounce this man."

She rose and paced the room, while I, following her agitated movements with my eye, in imagination pursued the dreadful consequences of the murderer's apprehension to their dire end. And yet, in my ignorance, I saw but the plainest, smallest portion of the horror and disgrace that would fall upon our family. What terrible events and secrets lay unknown which this man's trial would bring to light I guessed not, yet I could see enough to make my flesh creep, and my eyes close in horror with a sick shudder.

"It would kill my father," I ejaculated, in a low voice.

"I know it," answered Miss Admonitia, with a deep sigh, "yet that would not stay his hand for a single moment. He would stretch it out to seize this man, regardless alike of dragging down ruin and death upon himself and others. Silence, Esther, silence, that is our only hope, our only resource. We must leave the murderer to God, and entreat his forgiveness for ourselves if we sin in leaving him to Divine rather than human justice.

"Now," she continued, "let me speak of my reason for coming here to-day. I did not intend our talk should take this turn. Your father has had a long conversation with me, and he has also written fully to Mildred, on the subject of what he terms your delusions. It seems, since your illness, certain ideas remain fixed in your mind, and you cannot rid yourself of them. Then cease the endeavour, Esther; wonder, ponder, and read no more on the subject; fix your thoughts on other things, and these sickly fancies will fade away of themselves. I disapprove of all the books your father has put into your hands. You will get your mind into a morbid state with such studies, till you imagine yourself haunted, or afflicted like the epileptic, cataleptic, and crazy people of whom you are reading. Brain fever is simple enough, and when that passed away, and your health was restored, your memory became partially weakened, until change of air, quiet, and sounder health brought it back to you. There, that's the simple history of your case. Do you find anything very wonderful in it?"

"Certainly not, if that were all," I replied, in a puzzled way; "but the thing I saw on the roof, that papa affirms I never really saw, but only fancied — what of that?"

"What of that?" repeated Miss Admonitia, calmly. "I was not speaking of that as a delusion. I understood you had other fancies "—and here she looked at me searchingly. "I perceive nothing wonderful in your having seen our poor old demented servant, Sarah Tregellas."

"Sarah Tregellas!" I exclaimed, in amazement.

"Her stay at Treval was no secret to any one but you, Esther," said Miss Admonitia, with a faint smile. "Poor Sarah was my mother's maid, and Mildred and I felt bound to retain her with us, although she had conceived a strange dislike to us both—a dislike which, at one bitter time of our lives, induced her to do my sister all the injury in her power, which I need not tell you has gained for her a double kindness and tenderness from Mildred ever since. Never very amiable, Sarah grew childishly vindictive and mischievous in her old age, and in fact she was often dangerous; so we kept her in one of the upper rooms, in charge of a strong, kind nurse. When you came to us we thought there was enough in our ghostly old mansion to frighten you without letting you see, or hear of, poor Sarah. She was at times quite out of her mind, and she was bent nearly double, and had an odd way of creeping along, very ghostly to see to those not used to her, especially when one looked on her mindless, blank face. One thing I can promise you, Esther—she will never terrify you again; she is dead. She died a few nights ago of paralysis."

I remained silent, in a cloud of perplexed thought.

"I wish I had known this before," I murmured, softly.

"This is the first time I have seen you since your recovery," remarked Admonitia; "I don't see how I could have told you earlier. The moment we heard from Clifton, from your father, on what subject you raved during your illness, Mildred and I guessed you had seen Sarah, and we thought the best way to efface your terror was to let you see her every day. Familiarity soon ended the mischief that her apparition on the roof had caused you, though I confess it was a dangerous experiment, and you fainted the very first day we introduced you to Sarah at Treval. Still, every hour undid somewhat of the evil, till at last no one was a kinder nurse to the poor afflicted woman than you."

Miss Admonitia paused. Her brow contracted, her voice faltered, her eyes filled with tears, and it was only by an effort she continued her narrative.

"She was a faithful servant, with all her faults, and her death has grieved us, Esther. I am sorry, too, it should have happened before you had an opportunity of seeing her again. Now your memory is restored to you so clear and strong, the sight of her in all her reality would have completely effaced the dreamy, mysterious image which I fear your brain still retains. But surely you can remember somewhat of your last stay at Treval—you can recollect something of Sarah —something of what I am telling you?"

Miss Admonitia gazed at me with a searching look, and awaited my reply with a suppressed anxiety which I *felt* rather than saw.

"No, I can remember nothing," I answered, as I shook my head with a decided negative, as my mind made a vain effort to grope through that blank time. "If Jenifer had not told me, I should never have known I had been to Treval. Only, on my recovery, I found strangely effaced from my brain all terror of the figure I had seen. That is the sole result of my visit to you, Miss Admonitia."

"It is the only result needed," she answered, calmly—"the sole reward Mildred and I desired for our care."

"I — I feel I ought to thank you," said I, falteringly (but the truth was, I never could thank them — never could feel grateful for anything they did); "doubtless you and Miss Mildred had much trouble with me—much anxiety and fatigue."

"Do not force yourself to be grateful, Esther, when you don't feel it; and there is no need. We did nothing for you—of course not. We could not worry ourselves with a querulous sick girl. We left all that to Martha and the nurse we hired."

She spoke in that hard, dry, sneering tone which had always silenced me when a child. I rebelled against it now, and after a moment's pause for thought, I said, with a slight tinge of sarcasm—

"I presume you made papa aware of Sarah's existence from the first? How was it, then, that he did not simply inform me I had seen her, instead of arguing with me respecting delusions, and procuring me books to prove his assertions?"

Miss Admonitia's face flushed hotly, but

she met my gaze with a look of supreme disdain.

"So you have not yet discovered your father's great weakness—superstition? It is not in his nature to give you a true, commonplace explanation of a mystery. Nothing I can say will convince him that you saw Sarah — a poor, harmlessly-demented servant-woman. The figure you beheld has for him a far more wonderful signification; he believes his lost love, the murdered Alicia, appeared to you, and when he talks to you about delusions it is himself he is trying to soothe and persuade, not you. He scouts the idea of your having seen Sarah. He even refused to name her to you."

I was silenced. I felt to the inmost core of my heart that this was the truth with regard to my father's feelings; my own I could scarcely analyse yet.

"I am very weary of all this talk, Esther,"

said Miss Admonitia, and she put her hand to her head with a look of pain. "Sing me something as you used to do at Treval; it will do me good. There is your grandmother's harpsichord open, I see. Have you been playing?"

I looked at her in blank astonishment as she spoke, and my first thought was that she was mocking me cruelly.

"You know well," I answered, fiercely, "that I cannot play a note. You would not let me learn; and as to singing, you never heard me at Treval. I only sang when I hid in the wood or climbed the trees like a hunted bird. How can you say I ever sang to you at Treval?"

I spoke in a hot, angry tone; yet Miss Admonitia regarded me calmly, almost pitifully, and the tears again came to her eyes.

"You often climbed the cedar, Esther. Did you ever sing up there among those great dark branches?"

"No, I never sang there," said I, softened. "I was too frightened, too watchful then for—— Where did you keep Sarah? I used to see her from the cedar branches, yet I could never find her room."

So sudden and fearful a change came over Miss Admonitia's face that I started up and ran towards her, thinking she was ill. She waved me back with her hand, and faintly asked for a glass of water. I hurried away to fetch it, but when I returned the drawing-room was empty, and the roll of wheels echoed on the gravel. Running to the window, I saw the Treganowen carriage departing, and received the farewell wave of Miss Admonitia's pale white hand.

## CHAPTER V.

I can scarcely tell in what state of mind this visit and abrupt departure left me. I was so trammelled, so sickened, so walled round by the horrible fact that a murderer's blood ran through my veins, that I put off thought wearily, saying to myself that I would reflect when the red image of this man Paul grew fainter in my mind. I was not free now to think. It held me tightly, as in a vice, and chained all my faculties to the contemplation of its hideous presence.

When my father returned from his ride he found me still sitting dreamily by the window, looking out with fixed eyes upon the summer sea, which, languid with sunshine, lazily laved the shingle on the hot beach.

I roused myself to talk to him, and, by a great effort, dismissing from my mind the dominant figure of Paul now tyrannizing over every thought, I plunged into a crowd of questions bearing on the life and death of the woman Sarah Tregellas.

It was true that she had long lived in a feeble state of mind, kindly succoured and cared for at Treval—true that she was only just now dead and buried; but beyond this my father's statements and Miss Admonitia's no longer tallied. According to him, Sarah had long been confined to her bed, paralytic, and incapable of any exertion. To believe that she had crept along the roof from beam to beam the whole length of the western front was for him impossible. He was willing to think the figure a mysterious illusion, which he connected somehow with his approaching presence at Treval, but he would not admit it could have been Sarah. Perhaps his belief went further, and, fancying himself beloved by Alicia, he may have imagined his coming presence at the scene of his sorrow troubled the poor spirit, and raised her up to meet him, or induced her to show her pallid, woful face to his young daughter. Such thoughts have visited human hearts at times, and to some natures there is no pain and no fear in the fancy. Not to me, however, if he had such a thought, did he show it openly. He contented himself by saying—

"Perhaps Miss Admonitia's motive is good, but I consider she is combating the morbid impression on your brain dishonestly by a story incredible in itself. The braver course is always the safest, Esther, so I prefer to take it, honestly acknowledging all that is strange in the circumstance, while at the same time I put works into your hands which prove how common such delusions are during disease. Time will show who is the wiser—Miss Admonitia or I."

He left me with these words, and while he thus showed me his own leaning toward the mystic, proving the correctness with which Miss Admonitia's acute penetration had divined his failing, he forgot that he had flung my mind back into a state of doubt and pain, vacillating between the natural and the supernatural, the commonplace and the mysterious, while among these glimmered a third feeling—an instinct like a thread of light—leading me gradually on to the truth.

And yet it was only by crediting Miss Admonitia's statement that I could account for the singular familiarity and cessation of fear with regard to this creeping figure of which I was conscious in my own mind; hence I was inclined to believe her. I say inclined, because behind the inclination lurked a doubt, which grew and expanded, and at last burst into the light of certainty, in which light, when the time came, and my hand was older, I unlocked that secret on the roof, and found my own house not safe from the fear of it. Even now, after long lapse of years, when I remember that time, I am afraid, and trembling lays hold of my flesh. Let me speak of it in the right place. Why should I anticipate, in the history of my childhood, the terrors of my youth?

On the evening after Miss Admonitia's visit my father talked and read with me a long while; but, in spite of the feverish excitement and interest I felt in the books we perused together, and in his anecdotes of strange occurrences, every one of which found an echo within my nervous and mystic nature, there still ever loomed before me the red figure of the man—the murderer, Paul Polwhele. His relationship to me ran hot and loathingly through my veins; his face peered over my shoulder, his hand touched me at each instant, till my flesh quivered with hate and fear. It appeared to me that he was claiming me body and soul, and, though every fibre in my frame stirred against him with a separate loathing, yet I acknowledged the claim, and shrank and shivered before it helpless. At night, shut in my own room in utter loneliness, I grew worse. I shuddered at the horrible thoughts that crept round me like snakes; I cowered at a shadow; I trembled at every distant sound, till at length, overcome by the inert terror that had grown upon me, I flung myself on my knees by the bedside, with my head on my arms, and in this attitude I remained till my candle burnt down in the socket and went out, leaving me in darkness. Then, in an anguish of fear, still dressed as I was, I crept on to the bed and tried to sleep; but my fevered imagination peopled the room with phantom Pauls, each one murdering Alicia, each one claiming a horrid kin to me, and banishing sleep like the spectres that haunted Macbeth.

In the midst of the darkness and silence, while I was listening to the beating of my own heart, and striving to deaden the horrible wakefulness of my brain, our great door-bell sounded. It clanged and echoed through the sleeping house, breaking on the ear with a noise tenfold louder than it ever uttered by day, yet no one stirred. The sound rushed through every avenue of my sense, vibrating along the darkness and stillness with an unnatural clamour and life, and startling me from my unreal terrors into more human aud healthful fears. Just beneath my window stood a small platform of lead, forming the roof of the porch. It had lately by my wish been embellished by vases of growing flowers, which I tended myself, and I remembered now that from this place I could speak to the unwonted visitor, and bid him go to another door, as the bell at the great entrance was too far from the servants' apartments to give him a chance of awakening them. In a moment, with thoughts of disaster, sickness, fire, I know not what, I had opened the window, and stood with my white dress fluttering in the breeze peering downwards with anxious eyes for the midnight disturber of our rest. Whoever he was he had only rung once, but the champ and neigh of a horse beneath on the gravel assured me he had not departed.

"Who is there?" said I, loudly.

"Is it possible?—is that indeed you, Miss Esther? How sorry I am I have disturbed you!" answered a voice which brought my heart with a glad bound to my lips.

"Dr. Spencer!" I exclaimed, as I clasped my hands joyfully. "Why, they told me you had left England."

"Not yet," he replied, cheerfully.

" Oh, how shall I let you in ?" I cried. " I cannot undo the bolts of the great door, I am not strong enough, they are so hard. And, besides, I have no candle. Won't you go round to the other door, while I wake the servants?"

" There is no necessity for letting me in at all," said the doctor. " I would not have come, but I saw a light a moment ago in this window, and as it is not long past eleven, I had no idea of finding every one gone to rest but you. On the contrary, I expected to find all the household up excepting yourself, and I came, thinking to make you sleep all the happier by sending you this letter."

" A letter for me !" I exclaimed.

" Yes, from Miss Mildred. She wrote it at nine this evening, and the moment it was finished I started with it. How fortunate I should find you up ! But how is it,

Miss Esther, that, like a nightingale, you alone are awake?"

"Oh, I have been so miserable!" said I, earnestly—"so afraid!"

"I thought so," answered Dr. Spencer, softly. "Here is your letter: can you reach it?"

I bent down from the roof of the porch, and in the faint moonlight perceived the glimmer of the paper in his hand, which he held up towards me as high as he could reach. Still it was not high enough, and I stretched towards it in vain.

"I cannot get it," said I, sorrowfully, "so you had better bring it to me to-morrow."

"No, you are to have it and read it to-night, and then sleep in peace. Miss Mildred told me it would make you happier, so we'll try what a clamber can do."

In a moment or two, by some means, I found his hand within the grasp of mine, and I had the letter safe. I never thought now of the dark night, or of the loneliness, or of the terrible fears that lay scattered behind me; all became peace, and light, and life, as my slight cold fingers lay within the warm clasp of his hand.

"Do you know I cannot stand very long on this stony cherub?" said Dr. Spencer, laughing; "so please point out to me the fair Jenifer's window, and then I'll jump down."

"Jenifer's window! What do you want of Jenifer?"

"You said you had no light, and I suppose no flint and steel, so I want her to bring you a candle, that you may read your letter. I'll awaken her with a salute of gravel, and send her to you."

"No, no; you shall not take that trouble," I cried. "I'll read the letter to-morrow."

" Which is Jenifer's window, Miss Esther?"

" Oh, don't give yourself so much trouble about me!" I exclaimed, with tears in my voice. "I am not at all afraid now, and I shall sleep without reading the letter."

" Do you wish me to salute every window in the house with pebbles? Where does the fair Jenifer slumber?"

" How obstinate you are!" said I, smiling. " Turn to the right, and count the windows beneath the east turret: hers is the third."

" Good-bye, Miss Esther. You look like a fairy there all in white, standing among your flowers."

But though he said " Good-bye," I did not relinquish his hand.

" When will you come again?" said I, wistfully. " You have been away so long."

" I will come again to-morrow. And the

next time I go, I will take you with me if you like."

"Will you?" I exclaimed, with a sudden start of joy. "But no, I cannot leave papa."

"Then we'll carry him off too," said Dr. Spencer. "This cruel cherub won't bear me on his stony wings any longer. He is no angel, he is a veritable imp, thirsting for my life. Good night. He has not broken my neck, Miss Esther; I am safe."

This was in answer to my exclamation of alarm as he sprang down hastily on my relinquishing his hand.

With another merry "Good night" he mounted his horse and rode away to the right towards the east turret. By the light of the moon, just rising above the trees, and with the soft summer air blowing around me, I stood and watched him.

How beautiful the night was, how beautiful the sky with its quiet stars, how beautiful the fresh stillness of the air, the low murmur of the sea, and the gentle roll of the shaken pebbles as they wandered back with the returning waves, softly, like the sound of a last kiss! All breathed music, and fell about my spirit like a mantle of peace and loveliness; and the hot fret of fever that had run through my veins, the flush of fear, the burning dread and loathing that awhile ago had chafed me into such a fire of pain were all gone, quenched in this calm, fled away before the charm of a soothing word, and the touch of a kind human hand.

The dash of the gravel against Jenifer's window and the music of a pleasant voice reached me like new notes in the song the summer night now sang to my spirit. The echo of the horse's hoofs as he galloped away was like the beating of time to the measure, and every flower and every leaf answered the voices of the night in melody, as they sang out their carol to the silvery sea.

A flash of light from my window roused me from my listening happiness.

"Ah! it arn't nothing catching cowld now," said Jenifer complacently. "You may bide out there aal night ef you will, Miss Esther; et waient be aught but a pleasure to me, becaise I shall go arter tha doctor en tha mornin'. And ef you stops ill for a month, tha greater joy and satisfaction I shall have, Miss Esther; so don't 'ee come in 'pon no account."

Of course I had already entered the room and closed the window before Jenifer finished her oration.

"Well," she said, looking at me with a countenance beaming with delight, "how d'ye feel, Miss Esther?"

"I feel quite well, Jenifer, thank you."

"Es thic aal you've goet to say? And you doant feel like sunshine all over? nor like quickselver houlding tha pure gowld? nor like songs of birds running all through your heart? nor like a spring of water in tha sands? Ef you doant feel like all that, I do, Miss Esther."

"How can I feel like sunshine, Jenifer, when it's night?"

"Night!" exclaimed Miss Jenifer; "why, it's the beautifullest day to me that I ever see! Tha day broke tha minute I heerd *his* voice. 'Twas night yesterday, and every yesterday sence the sun sit tha hour he went away. I thought I were dreaming when I heerd the cry, 'Jenifer! Jenifer!' sweet as a grey-bird's whistle tuning in at my window. Then when it comed clearer my heart tumbled upside down, and I felt as ef a live cunger wes in my throat murdering me weth chokes, for I maade sure he wes dead, I ded. And he's come to tell *me*, I says to myself, bekase he knows I likes his very shadder better than I likes any other man's four bones. He knows ef I wes a princess, rech as butter, cloathed in bank-notes, with guineas to walk upon, I couldn't get up no greater dance en my heart than I does now, whenever hes bright faace comes ento my two eyes. Well, in a minute I hears 'Jenifer! Jenifer!' again, and a thoomping pebble at my winder crazed a squeer, so then I knowed 'twas his very self en tha warm flesh. And ef you'd only seed, Miss Esther, how quick I goet my head out ef winder, and how in waun instant I felt oop to tha roots of my hair in honey, and balm, only weth the first glint I had en tha moonlight of his comfortable smile—a smile, Miss Esther, that would slock\* me ento a whirpool arter 'un———"

"Now, Jenifer," I interrupted, "will you be quiet and let me read my letter?"

"Ah! it's a letter from thic wisht ould white raven at Treval, esn't et?" said

\* *Slock* is to entice.

Jenifer, drily. " I never see sich a oogly ould terror in aal my boarn days, n't I. She's like a bundle of dried bones rustling about in a silken garment. I should be skeered to touch ort b'longing to her."

Nevertheless, Jenifer, to whom all writing was a cabalistic and unknown mystery, peered over my shoulder curiously as I read these words:—

" MY DEAR CHILD, — Admonitia has grieved me by confessing that, in her anger, she told you of your relationship to Paul. I cannot deny this truth, though I would give much to have spared you the pain of knowing it. But one sorrow—the most terrible—I can completely lift from your heart. Admonitia is mistaken, your mother is mistaken : Paul's hand never touched my sister. He is innocent of that blood. Believe me, I *know* that he is innocent. If I did not know it should I let him go free ?

It is to avoid uselessly laying bare to the eyes of a gaping world all this ghastly history of blood and sorrow that I refuse to pursue this man. Why should I dig up my sister's name from its grave? why rack your father's heart? why disgrace him, you, and your mother by arresting an innocent man? —innocent, I mean, of this crime, though many other guilty deeds of his would doubtless come to light, sufficient to overwhelm you all with shame and pain. Never fear, Esther, I shall not touch him. Sleep in peace. Paul Polwhele's hand is innocent as mine of the blood of my sister; whatever his crimes may be, the murder of Alicia Tremaine is not one of them. I say this who know it.

"Your friend and mother,
"MILDRED TREMAINE."

An immense weight seemed taken off my heart as I read this strange letter, and a feeling of gratitude for the first time softened my hard thoughts of Miss Mildred.

"Aw! my dear Miss Esther," said Jenifer, rousing me abruptly from the soothing thankfulness and relief in which I was steeped, "what a bufflehead I be! While you've bin reading I've bin thinking whether you couldn't teach me to write, and make me a lady."

"I'll teach you to write if you like, Jenifer."

"But you caent make me a lady, miss?" responded Jenifer, with a sigh.

"Are you not happy as you are, Jenifer?"

"I think if I wes a dog I'd be happier. When is he coming again, Miss Esther?"

"To-morrow, Jenifer."

"That's a blessing, any way. But what a long night this 'll be! I think when you're in bed, Miss Esther, I'll go out and sit on the white gate-post at the end of tha revenue."

"What on earth for, Jenifer?" said I, laughing.

"I shall see tha fust of 'un then as he comes oop tha road."

"Why, Jenifer, he may not come till eleven or twelve o'clock to-morrow."

"That needn't hender me from sitting on tha post, miss. Thic's no time for a dog to wait. I've seed our Trim wait a whole day for master. Miss Esther," continued Jenifer, solemnly, "I reckon sure I'm turning into a dog, I've growed that watchful, and steady, and patient, and I'm thankful for so little. A croom of kindness makes me feel like walking to the world's end to pay 'un, a look puts a laugh ento all my veins, and ef he aunly stands en my eyesight for a minute I'm as grateful as I am for sunshine. My eyes feel warm and alight, filled up weth his face. It does me so much good to look at 'un, that ef I had tha rechest mine en tha county, I'd give all tha ore, fast as it comed to grass, only to pay 'un for standing somewheres every day where I could see 'un for two minutes. Is that like a dog, Miss Esther?"

"Something, Jenifer," said I, sleepily, as I laid my head on the pillow.

"I could talk till sunrise, but you are tired, so good night, miss. If I was a lady like you, growing up beautiful like you," said Jenifer, wistfully, turning as she reached the door, "I'd love 'un not like a dog, but like a woman."

## CHAPTER VI.

I stole, early in the morning, into our great drawing-room, and seated myself in a huge arm-chair, where my small form seemed quite lost, swallowed up as it were by the mass of oak and damask on which I sat. Those were the days when scanty garments neither hid a grace nor gave one, so no voluminous folds of drapery or cumbrous crinoline magnified the diminutive proportions of my tiny figure as I leant back in the crimson chair, with feet scarcely touching the ground.

My pen is soon about to quit this period of my life, but ere it leaves Esther Treganowen the child, let it endeavour to draw her picture for you.

Imagine a small oval face, intensely white, crowned by a mass of waving chestnut hair, so long and thick that it was a marvel, a forehead too massive for the thin cheeks, a mouth too firm for a child, and eyes so strange and solemn that I was afraid at times to meet them in the glass. I had a fancy that it was these witch-like eyes that kept me companionless, that made the servants whisper together about me, that caused strangers to call me old, or talk of elves and pixies when I passed. The peculiar expression they held I can only convey to your mind by the word *lost;* a lost look swam in their deep darkness, painful, searching, mysterious, which stirred the heart with an emotion half fear, half wonder. Hence people as they gazed became conscious of wild thoughts concerning me, floating doubts and surmises which touched on all that is mystic and strange in our nature. Let me add that one glance from these eyes of mine instantly destroyed indifference. I was liked or disliked at once —oftenest the last—for they excited an intense curiosity. I was seen to be a secret a something to unravel, and where curiosity exists indifference dies. The setting of these orbs, their brows and lashes, were raven-black, making a strange contrast with my hair, which seemed to hold a sunbeam running through its darkness, giving warmth to my face, and taking from it the chill look which the intense whiteness of my complexion would otherwise have lent to it. Yet even this sunniness of hair helped to give me a strange look, for in shadow the heavy tresses appeared almost black, while in light they gleamed with a golden lustre like a glancing fire. I seemed a witch wearing some unholy halo; and in after days a voice I dearly loved would often call to me playfully to come out of the sunlight and quench the sorceress's fire dancing around my head.

Do you know me now, or can you only bring before your eyes the aged Esther, whose blanched hair and familiar figure bear for you no mystic gleam, and whose calm face, humanized by many a line of sorrow, shows that suffering is the link that binds all human beings together, and makes the rarest nature akin to the commonest?

Let us be thankful for grief: it humanizes, it destroys the dreamy, selfish egotism round which imagination, in never-tiring coils of self-exalting thought, winds long silken threads of reverie, bright with golden riches, all heaped up before the idol self. Suffering throws this false god down, and leads the soul to the worship of the true, and all the treasures of the spirit offered once on the hideous altar of self, where they dwindled or rankled into sin, are poured out now in a full tide of blessing to others.

Tenderness, pity, love flow forth from the wounded heart given to God, and peace follows. The Shadow of the Fall, with its mystic pain, its look not human, full of unreason, lost, fades from the brow, and, looking on the face of one thus redeemed, we behold it as the face of a MAN.

O my children, for whom I write, if in these withered features, careworn and aged, you see only the face of a *woman*, let me hope that sorrows have not passed over me in vain, and that I do well to say, let us be thankful for grief!

See how far behind in memory Esther the aged, while she sketched her portrait, has left the child-girl seated in the armchair. Long ago I entreated your pardon for these garrulous breaks in an old woman's narrative, so I make no new apology as I gather up the dropped thread of my story.

For whom was I waiting thus in silent watchfuess, my nerves athrob with expectation? Not for the hero of that golden web which day by day my fancy wove in radiant colours. Flashing into the mirror of hope there came a face illumined by romance, which imagination exalted into the place of worship. The kind, the homely, the true, the tender were too near, too easy of reach, and my heart passed them over to yearn after the unattainable. Nevertheless, there was something so thoroughly human and sympathetic in Dr. Spencer's nature, that, dazzled as I was by the image of my own romance, I could not remain unresponsive to its magnetic influence. I can only truly describe him in the homely words used by Shakspeare in depicting such another character—"He was kind and *comfortable.*" And, yielding to this indescribable charm of comfort, home, ease, my shut-up spirit ventured to leave its shy loneliness, and warmed itself in the joy that seemed to glow around his presence like an atmosphere. My frozen heart thawed in this radiance of life and love, flowing from the generous fountain of his soul like light flows from the sun, freely, spontaneously, unconsciously; no wonder, then, was it that, all aglow with joy and hope, it beat now with happy throbs, expecting him.

Not daring to speak to my father of Miss Mildred's letter, lest he should ask to see it, I had dreaded to mention the doctor's visit; and finding in the morning that none knew of it but Jenifer and myself, I remained silent altogether, glad thus to escape questioning. Hence it was that my father had gone out ignorant that a visitor was expected, and I sat alone in the great drawing-room, with the sunshine just turning to flame the crimson damask of the chair, and lighting up the sorceress's wavy fire that crowned my white face. With my small thin hands clasped and lying on my lap, I sat with outward patience, a thousand hot thoughts throbbing in my brain, and one strong purpose ever coming nearer and clearer from out the mist of dreams and darkness in which I lived. A hurried step, and my heart leapt with a glad bound, escaping from this haze of thought into the sunshine, as Jenifer dashed into the room breathless, exclaiming—

"Miss Esther, he's coming!—he es! But he's fine and wisht looking, and changed, sure enough. I'm bedoled to see 'un, I be. Ax 'un what's the matter, Miss Esther, wont 'ee!"

With a deep sigh and a rapid pantomime of amazement and distress, Jenifer made her escape a moment before the doctor entered. He regarded me with great earnestness, and —I could not help the passing fancy—with somewhat of the same curiosity with which a botanist examines a specimen of rare plant or flower; then he bowed to me gravely, and sat down opposite, like a visitor waiting to be entertained by his hostess. I kept my hands folded on my lap, and surveyed him with equal dignity.

"Have you had a pleasant ride hither, Dr. Spencer?"

"Very, Miss Treganowen, thank you."

"Did you come over this morning from Treval?"

"Not from Treval, but from Trevalla Church-town, as you say here, where I have been staying with my uncle, Mr. Winterdale."

I was conscious of a start of surprise flushing my face, but I only said, quietly—

"Is Mr. Winterdale your uncle?"

"He is my mother's brother, Miss Esther."

The flush died out of my face, and I grew pale, paler than my own natural pallor, as his words brought, like a flash of sharp fire, the red image of Paul to my eyes. I heard his next words indistinctly, as we hear things in pain and sickness.

"Did that letter make you happier last night?"

"Yes, thank you, it made me much happier."

I could not help the look of pain, the deep sigh with which I spoke.

"Then it was really a kindness in Miss Mildred to write it?" said the doctor, doubtfully.

My eyes met the searching glance of his with a sudden, sharp sympathy. We both, then, suspected Miss Mildred—justly or unjustly—of something.

"Yes, it was *really* a kindness."

"I am glad of it," answered the doctor. "But as I was bringing the letter, I was undecided whether I would fling it into the sea or deliver it into your hands, especially as I was bidden on no account to give it to the colonel. Have you shown it to him this morning, Miss Esther?"

"I have not said a word to him," I replied, as a painful sensation rose in my throat. "Please not to speak of the letter to papa; it would hurt him to know anything about it."

An impatient movement of the hand expressed the doctor's vexation.

"Secrets between your father and you, Miss Esther!"

"It is not my fault if they tell me to be secret. And, then, if it would *hurt* my father to know?"

I felt my anxious look of unchildish thought and fear was withering my face into age as I spoke, and a something too painful for words quivered in the unnatural tones of my young voice. The doctor was touched with pity; he rose suddenly, then sat down again.

"Poor child!" he murmured; "the

crown flames with sharp torture, I see. Come out of that sorcerer's fire, Miss Esther, which makes you look like a witch at the stake, and sit here by me. There is a sinister portrait frowning above you, with a ban on his lips, as though he rejoiced in that bristling atmosphere of pain which, to my fancy, flames around you there. Come and face him, and defy him from this place at my side."

It was the same Treganowen whose scowling face had looked down on my mother as she slept, when her brother, full of treachery and theft, stole upon her out of the darkness, and I thought of this scene as I obeyed the doctor, changing my seat to one by his side on the sofa.

"This is a good change," he said, smiling and patting my cheek. "The fire has died out from these rippling waves of hair, and they are nearly black now. I like them best thus. So we must obey—say nothing about her letter?"

"For papa's own sake," I faltered.

I looked up and caught the doctor's deep grey eyes fixed earnestly, searchingly on my face. It was not the first time I had met that glance, half penetrating, half compassionate, and my gaze fell before it.

"They burden and torture your young mind with secrets," he said, "as carelessly as if no sickness, no disease ever grew out of an over-tried brain."

"Perhaps they cannot help it," said I, sorrowfully, as I thought of the chain of circumstances that had led to one strange mystery after another, crowding into my knowledge.

"Let us hope they cannot," he answered, gravely.

Shrinking from the thought of Paul, ever hovering near me in this talk, I abruptly changed the conversation.

"You are much altered, Dr. Spencer; have you been ill?" I asked.

"I have been suffering a little, but I am quite well now," he answered, carelessly.

I have said, that it was not till after a lapse of years that I became acquainted with the true circumstances of his illness, and long absence from Treganowen. Fearing any new shock might attack my still trembling health, all had been carefully kept secret from me, and, indeed, the fact of his being wounded was known only to his uncle and his old housekeeper. The villagers and his friends, including my father, were simply told that he was ill, and even this information was not granted to poor Jenifer. Fearing the discretion of her tongue in her long conferences with me, she was merely told that he had left Treganowen; hence her idea that he was gone to "furrin parts."

On how slight a thread hangs our fate!

Had Dr. Spencer divulged the truth to me now, it must have been followed by implicit confidence on my part, and the web which we took so many years to unravel might have been cut in a day. But he turned lightly from the subject of his changed looks, saying with a smile—

"So you thought I was gone abroad again, and I hear you never even asked for me."

"I asked Jenifer," said I, blushing deeply, and then laughing a little.

"What does that laugh mean?" demanded the doctor.

But I shook my head and gave him no answer. And as I reflected on poor Jenifer's eccentric devotion, and the ease and unwittingness with which he had gained it, the thought struck me that his was one of those happy natures that attract, destined to be loved everywhere without effort, while mine repelled, and I might give "all the substance of my house for love and it would avail me nothing."

"Jenifer likes you very much," said I, sadly. "No one will ever like me."

"My poor child," answered the doctor, "you fancy so because you have never lived with any *human beings* since you were born. No wonder you look a thousand years old, and your little face is white and solemn as a sibyl's."

I glanced at him as he spoke, and as his grey eyes, flashing into a smile, lit up with the "summer lightning of a soul full of summer warmth," it seemed to me that his was the brightest, sunniest face I had ever seen, and so young, so much younger than mine, though I was fourteen and he was twenty-four.

I gave him back his smile, and then I clasped my fingers together nervously, and looked at him with great eyes fixed and solemn.

"You are thinking that if you are very old I am very young, and you are afraid to say it."

I nodded assent, then as I continued my rapt gaze, a slight quiver came into my lips, as I felt a sort of wonder stealing over me at sight of so much youth and happiness. I had never seen it before, never known it.

"You are quite right, Miss Esther," said the doctor, his whole face breaking into a play and flash of merriment—"my age is ten. Let us have a game of battledore and shuttlecock. No, not here in this room. We should batter the noses of the family portraits, and that wouldn't be respectful. Out there, please, in that pretty court, where the fountain is playing with the sunshine."

"If you like," said I, timidly, rather thinking battledore and shuttlecock beneath my dignity; but I was not of this opinion long. It was a magic wand the doctor wielded, not a battledore, and we played, and laughed, and shouted, and talked till my eyes sparkled, and my veins ran with new life, and my wan cheeks flushed healthfully, and a child grew out of the game with whom the weird, wistful Esther Treganowen was but too little acquainted.

If I talked and laughed, the doctor talked and laughed more. He never flagged a moment, but kept the shuttlecock flying in the midst of scattered jests, and glee, and anecdotes, which came pouring from his tongue musically, like a sparkling waterfall of words.

"There goes the shuttlecock in the fountain, Miss Esther, which shows your arm is tired at last. I think I could eat some peaches—could you?"

"Yes, and I'll ring——"

"No, you won't. We'll go into the garden and gather them ourselves."

## CHAPTER VII.

We strolled into the garden as happily as though no unnatural care or terror had ever sat upon my heart; and we gathered peaches, we shook down and wasted plums, pears, and apricots till we drove the gardener wild, while our jests and laughter rang high up into the summer air, and the little birds twittered in the branches in mimic emulation of our merriment.

It was long past noon when we came in by the small door under the east turret, and I caught a glimpse of Jenifer's face peering over the winding stairs, beaming with such admiring worship and happiness that I could not repress a smile.

"Another sly laugh!" exclaimed the

doctor, "and you will not tell me what it means?"

"It means that Jenifer thinks you the best and handsomest man in the world."

"And you laugh at her, when you ought rather to admire her good taste and excellent sense! Jenifer!" he called, "don't run away—we want you."

"Can I bring you some lunch, sir?" asked Jenifer, in great confusion.

"I never refuse anything nice," said the doctor; "so if you have something very good that Miss Esther and I shall like you may bring it."

Radiant with delight, Jenifer soon laid before us cold partridge and tongue, a dish of honeycomb clear as amber, a cluster of grapes, a plate of purple figs, and a bowl of clouted cream, the whole flanked by a bottle of Admiral Treganowen's old Madeira.

"Jenifer, I look upon you as a genius," said the doctor, helping me with that care and pleasure which make one glad to eat. " Do you think you and I and Miss Esther could live together comfortably ? "

" 'Twould be going to heaven afore one's time," said Jenifer, in a fiery glow of delight.

" Not a bit of it Jenifer ; I'm a domestic tyrant. In whatsoever house I find myself, there I'm master for the time being. Even the cat has to give way to me. If I took a fancy to the place where she lay curled up on the hearth-rug I should turn her out and take it. In fact, I will have my own way everywhere."

" But yours es such a nice way, sir," said Jenifer, "that every one likes you to have it."

After which speech, being excessively frightened at her boldness, Jenifer hid behind the doctor's chair, and made imploring gestures to me for permission to depart; but he, sympathetic as iron to the magnet, divined her wish instantly.

"No, Jenifer, you cannot go—we want you to wait at table. We hate the men-servants—that is, Miss Esther does; one is too soft-footed—the Indian—and walks like a cat, and we — that is, Miss Esther—always think he is going to spring on her; and the other is too heavy-footed, and walks like an elephant, and we—Miss Esther again—expect every moment to be trampled on and crushed."

"How can you know exactly the nonsense I think?" said I, getting very red.

"I wish all your thoughts were as easy to read as these," answered the doctor. "Now, I know it would be good for your health if every secret of your heart were poured in here"—touching his ear, which was wonderfully small, and shaped like a little pink sea-shell—" but while you are in this fortress you will not do it, for which reason I intend to take you and Jenifer to live with me."

Here Jenifer made such a comical face of surprise and joy that I leant back in my chair and laughed aloud.

"And when I have you in my own house," continued the doctor, not permitting himself to be interrupted by my laughter—"in my own house, where I am the master of all, down to the tiniest mouse that squeaks— and he doesn't squeak without my leave— you'll soon come of your own accord, and ask me to read you as I read a book; and immediately after you have deposited every secret into my keeping, that solemn, sorceress mask you wear on your face will drop off, the flames that creep through your hair will die out, the wandering, lost look in your eyes will change to——"

"Peace and love found at last," broke in Jenifer; and then she immediately stopped, nigh scared to death at her own audacity.

"Really, Jenifer, you are very intelligent," observed the doctor. "I could not have finished better myself. What do you say? —do you care enough for Miss Esther to go with her?"

"Jenifer does not care for me," said I; "at least, she did not till you tended and nursed me. She has cared since."

The doctor took this as easily as he took everything else.

"Ah, well," he said, "then Jenifer will come to oblige me. Jenifer, you see that little girl there, so small that her wisdom surprises us, like the loud song of a tiny bird, that makes us wonder how so small a thing can hold so big a sound—well, she is *my* bird, a little bird that I tended back to life when it lay fluttering in death's grasp, and therefore I love it. A rare bird of curious plumage, Jenifer—sombre feathers above, bright beneath—a bird that gives songs in the night——"

"What can he mean?" I thought.

"——That startle some ears, but please mine. Will you come, Jenifer, and guard my bird from all cats and other evil things?"

"Especially them cats at Treval," said Jenifer.

The doctor, I fancied, started slightly, but he permitted Jenifer to continue.

"In coorse, sir, I'll go to the world's end ef you like."

"And if I go away, will you watch over her as a faithful dog would?"

"Well, it sims I am to be a dog, sure enough," murmured Jenifer, "sence he caals me one his awn self. I'll do that same, sir, sence you ask et."

"And if she should sing in the night, or fly away to some distant land, returning very sad and weary, Jenifer, you'll promise me never to be *afraid* of my birdie again?"

Jenifer turned pale, and looked at me with a strange glance; then she scanned the doctor's face, and replied hurriedly—

"There esn't nothing as *you* don't know, sir. There, ef 'twas fire and waeter as I had to wade through, or mountains full of wild beasties and snakes to climb, ef you axed me I should go, sir; so I promise, though Miss Esther is a wisht bird to tend at times."

"Thank you for your promise, Jenifer; you'll keep it, I know. You are a good girl, and henceforth I put you on my list of friends, and shall guard a place for you in my memory, that no one wiser, or richer, or more beautiful shall ever take away."

And so saying, the doctor stretched out his hand to Jenifer, further rewarding her by a look from his marvellous eyes and a smile from his kind lips, for which, I feel sure, could she have performed any impossible task—such as walking round the world upon her head, or permitting hot steaks to be cut out of her body, like an Abyssinian cow—she would immediately have done it. As it was, she hurried away with her little pert nose excessively red, for all the tears she dared not let fall got into the tip and stung it.

"Poor Jenifer!" said I, when she was gone. "Why do you make her so fond of you?"

"I?" cried the innocent doctor—"I have not done anything in the world to make her fond of me. Would you have me beat her, Miss Esther, or treat her like a dog?"

"There is nothing she'd like better," said I, laughing. "The fact is, you certainly ought to be obliged to wear a mask: your face is a sort of trap to catch hearts."

"No, it only catches sunbeams."

"And sends them forth again," said I

"Ah!" at fourteen you pay me compliments," said the doctor, smiling; "at seventeen, like the cuckoo in June, you will change your note, and your opinion too, doubtless. Old as you are, Miss Esther, in your solemn ways, you are still child enough to give me your thoughts naïvely now; but what a closed book you will be to me then!"

His words flushed my face with a sudden red, and I caught up the apple rind which my fingers had shaped into an S, and threw it carelessly into my plate; then I changed the conversation abruptly.

"Is all this you have been saying a jest?" I asked; "or are you in earnest?"

"I am in earnest. I want you to come to Clifton to live with me and my mother. Her brother has already written to her about you!"

His mother's brother! The words echoed mournfully in my ears, like a spirit-voice whispering of Paul Polwhele. Oh! if I had told Dr. Spencer of this man now, and he had been candid with me, not fearing my childish years, what misery we should have spared each other!

But this was not to be till the appointed time, and until many a false light had led us both astray.

"Your father," continued the doctor, "has been consulting with Miss Tremaine on the propriety of sending you to school. But a school would not do for you, Miss Esther; I told Miss Mildred so last night."

"A school!" I exclaimed, and I felt my heart stand still at the thought. I, who had never had a companion, to be thrown among thirty or forty strange girls, to be subject to their curiosity and constant presence! I shrank from the idea as one would shrink from the rack. Moreover, my life of freedom, loneliness, and wild thought would render the restraints, the monotony, and routine of a school maddening to me.

"I should die," said I, simply, looking into the doctor's face with my eyes full of fear.

"I have no doubt of it," answered Dr. Spencer, in a tone of quiet conviction. "A fashionable boarding-school would be a cruel cage for such a bird as you. What would they do with you, I wonder?"

And he seemed amused by some thought in his own mind.

"In a week you would mystify the whole establishment; in a month you would be looked upon as a sort of witch, and be avoided by everybody."

"They would all hate me, I know," said I, sadly. "But I should not trouble them long; I should die. Yet why should I think of it? Papa will not send me."

"But Miss Mildred will," said the doctor.

I turned my pale face towards him, and

my heart trembled. I felt my father had no power against Miss Mildred's will.

"But you will save me," said I putting my hand into the doctor's, and looking into his eyes beseechingly.

"Fold your wings little bird; you have a safe nest here." He put his arm around me as he spoke. "You shall not die, and you will not be hated when you are with my mother and me."

I clung to him, and hid my face on his shoulder. I was so small, so fearful and fluttering, that I nestled within his sheltering arm truly like a frightened bird, and felt soothed and calmed as he stroked my hair and spoke to me gently.

"And will Miss Mildred let me go with you?" I asked.

"Wonder of wonders, she consents! She relaxes her grim hold on you for three years, at the end of which time you are to return to Treval. That is her bargain with me."

"How did you get her consent?" I cried, astonished.

"It was not I who got it, it was Mr. Winterdale. He went up to Treval and saw Miss Mildred himself."

"Saw Miss Mildred!" My amazement took away my breath. "Why, they never saw each other's faces when I was at Treval."

"They saw each other a few days ago," answered the doctor, smiling. "And I suppose my uncle has some powerful spell to subdue the strong will even of an enchantress like Miss Mildred, for, as I tell you, she consented, although last week I found her hard as a rock. She had fixed on some school at Exeter, kept by an old lady related to the Polwheles, and with this person she relied on your being kindly treated and highly educated, and she would hear of your going nowhere else. It seems she is just as anxious now for you to become accomplished as she was once to deny you all accomplishments, so you must work hard, for I have promised her great results from your three years' stay at Clifton."

All this was so strange, so unexpected to me, that I felt bewildered, and asked no more questions.

"My chief reason for wishing you to come with us——" But here the doctor stopped embarrassed, and looked at me searchingly. Perhaps my face in its blank wonder gave him the answer he needed, for he continued now without hesitation, "The reason is that my mother has already in her charge a young lady whose companionship will do you good. It was her presence, however—which I *know* will be so beneficial to you—that made Miss Mildred's great objection to your joining our household, an objection which seemed insuperable till Mr. Winterdale overcame it."

I did not answer. I was thinking, and my thoughts vexed me. The fact is, I did not like this interference of Mr. Winterdale in my affairs. I felt it as an indignity offered to my father.

"Your uncle appears to be a very persuasive man," said I, drily.

"I cannot explain his influence with Miss Mildred," answered the doctor.

"But it is rather singular he should interest himself in my affairs and in this other young lady's too, for I remember now you told me in the garden your mother, at Mr. Winterdale's persuasion, had taken charge of a little girl of my age."

"In her case he did it to oblige your father."

As Dr. Spencer uttered these words my heart beat rapidly with a sudden suspicion, and my lips trembled.

"Her name is Alice!" I exclaimed, fiercely. "And I hate that girl!"

"You hate her!" repeated the doctor, in a voice of surprise and pain.

"I hate her!" said I, decidedly, in a cool, hard tone.

"Why?" asked Dr. Spencer, and I could not but notice the intense expectation and eagerness of his look as he awaited my answer.

"How can I tell you why?" I replied, impatiently. "I feel that I hate her, that's enough."

"Is it possible you can remember anything about her?" he demanded, with his hand on my wrist, as though my pulse had a tongue to tell him.

"I recollect nothing," said I, uneasily, for I feared his penetration would probe deep as that old ash-root in the garden; "but I know I saw this girl at Bath. Jenifer told me that, and also that she was an orphan left in my mother's charge by a friend in India. For days, weeks, as I was getting better, I waited for my father to give me some information respecting this adopted child, whom my mother loves better than she loves me, but he has never spoken, and I have been too proud to ask questions."

Tears were in my eyes as I finished, but I felt defiance, hatred, and jealousy vibrating through my frame, rustling the very hair on my head like creeping fires, as I proudly brushed the tears away.

"I believe it is true," said Dr. Spencer, sadly, "that your mother regards Miss Weston with a singular affection; yet it is not to be wondered at: she is a loveable and beautiful girl."

My heart swelled almost to bursting, but I made no reply.

"And your father has never told you that he is her guardian?"

"No."

I did not add that, in the pride and

secretiveness of my nature, I had scorned to mention to him this unknown Alice, perhaps preferring the mystery which left me free to brood in gloomy surmising and hatred over her name.

"She is with my mother now, as Colonel Treganowen deemed it his duty to place her with some lady who—who——"

Dr. Spencer seemed searching for some expression he could not find.

"Who would not spoil and ruin her as mamma did," said I, bitterly.

"Well, Mrs. Treganowen kept her up late and her health suffered, that was it, I believe. Do you really dislike her so much that her presence will be disagreeable to you? If so, I am truly sorry, for it was my obstinacy on this point which overruled even Miss Mildred's adamant will."

I looked into his face for an explanation, and he continued with, I thought, a slight embarrassment of manner—

"Miss Esther, you have never had a companion, I believe you have never even spoken to a child, in your life."

"Except Tom Pengrath."

The doctor smiled and went on.

"Well, of all the needs for which your spirit thirsts, the need of companionship is the keenest; therefore, when my uncle made certain requests of me—never mind what—I insisted, as the strictest article of our treaty, that Miss Weston and you should be companions under my mother's roof, and, unless he gained Miss Mildred's consent to this, I refused, with all the pertinacity of my nature, to—in fact, to make myself agreeable to him in any way. I prided myself the more on my victory because he and Miss Mildred, antagonistic in all else, were, unknown to each other, secretly of accord in this. They both wished you to be alone at my mother's, and it was only my firmness that gained the day."

This explanation both irritated and bewildered me. What right had Mr. Winterdale to interfere in my affairs? I could brook Miss Mildred's most galling chain with more patience than I could bear even a touch from him. I did not care to go to his sister's now, and Alice Weston's presence would be no comfort or privilege to me. I scorned the thought.

"And had my father no voice in the disposal of his only daughter?" said I, with my lips trembling.

"Oh, Esther," answered Dr. Spencer, in a sorrowful tone, "how you mistake me! Should I presume to act without his wish? Miss Mildred is not aware of it, neither is my uncle; but my obstinacy on this point was prompted as much by what I saw was his most eager desire as by my own conviction that this young lady's presence would increase your happiness. In a letter which I wrote to him immediately on my recovery from—from that sickness which you say has changed me, I reminded him of the wonderful benefit you derived during your illness from the companionship of his ward, and I proposed you should be educated together at my mother's. The eagerness with which he seized my proposal showed how much it pleased him, and the sorrow with which he expressed his conviction that no power on earth would ever gain Miss Mildred's consent to it induced me to make use of my uncle as the lever to move her iron will. How I have fought, how immovable and obstinate I have been, you do not know, Miss Esther. And now you render my victory useless by telling me you hate Miss Weston."

He paused for my reply, but I remained a moment in deep thought. What he had just said altered considerably the phase of the question. Miss Mildred, then, openly desired I should be companionless at Mrs.

Spencer's. Mr. Winterdale secretly wished it, and if both were overruled by the superior firmness of Dr. Spencer, this he assured me was only exerted because he instinctively divined my father's wishes. It was victory to thwart both Miss Mildred and Mr. Winterdale; it was empire to please my father and myself. I began to waver in my feelings respecting Alice.

"Well, must I send Miss Weston away?" asked Dr. Spencer, sadly. "You have but to speak."

"You would not send her away to please me," said I, in a low tone.

"Would I not?" answered the doctor, smiling. "Miss Alice Weston has the health and spirits of a colt; she does not *want* me—you do. Moreover, she has a hundred friends—you have but three or four."

"And who are they?" I asked.

"Your father, Jenifer, myself, and Prudence White."

I noticed his omission of my mother's name, as well as Miss Admonitia's and Miss Mildred's; but I passed them over when I spoke.

"And why not put Mr. Winterdale on my list of friends?" said I.

Dr. Spencer's face flushed painfully.

"My uncle is rather eccentric," he said, "in his likes and dislikes."

I was certain he hated me, and I wanted nothing more now to assure me that he had some end in view, not friendly, when he persuaded Miss Mildred to place me with his sister.

"Well, is Miss Weston to go or stay?" said the doctor, abruptly.

Now that the choice was left to me, I could not help confessing that I had a burning curiosity in my heart to see this Alice who could "play, and sing, and speak French," and who was as tall as the notch in the old ash-root against which I had measured my small stature so often this summer.

"Do you think I shall like her?" said I, evasively.

"You loved her very much when you were ill at Bath, where she nursed you like a sister, and I feel sure you will love her again, and find her companionship a great pleasure. Your father is delighted at the thought of your being together. Now we have conquered Miss Mildred, who stood against us like adamant, will you make our victory of no avail by refusing to be this young lady's friend? Will you cause your father so bitter a disappointment?"

"No," said I, and I put my hand in the doctor's. "It will seem very strange to me to be with a girl of my own age. I shall be frightened. I don't think I shall like *this* Alice, but I will try."

"Esther!" said my father's voice.

There was something so exquisitely

painful in its cadence, that I looked up startled. He was standing in the doorway contemplating us, with a face so pale, so wrung as if by some sharp agony, that my words were arrested on my lips. I ran towards him, then stopped, for he had sunk into a chair and covered his face with his hand. There was a moment's deep silence —a silence so painful that I felt it in every nerve of my frame, yet could in no way understand its meaning. Dr. Spencer walked to the window, and stood there looking out upon the garden. I put my hand shyly, timidly on my father's arm; he looked up, and, suddenly drawing me towards him, kissed me.

"Has Dr. Spencer told you I am going away soon, Esther?" he said, in his old tone of voice.

"I have told her the arrangement you have made for her stay with Mrs. Spencer," said the doctor, looking round, "but not the reason that rendered it necessary."

I stood trembling, glancing from one to the other."

"Esther, my regiment is ordered to Lisbon, and I join it there immediately. I have not dared to tell you this before; I thought it would grieve you too much. For some time Admonitia and I have been debating the subject of your education, and while I still had to combat Mildred's desire to send you to school at Exeter, I would not say a word to you; but now that we have made so happy an arrangement for your future, I no longer fear to tell you that I am obliged to go. But I give you another companion, one of your own age, whom I hope you will love very much."

My father stooped hurriedly and kissed me again. Stunned by the sad news he gave me, I clung to him without speaking.

"Now go, my dear; I have much to say to Dr. Spencer."

I bade adieu to the doctor, and hastened away, agitated, trembling. While I had been dreaming listlessly, never marking the daily course of events, all this had been decided concerning me. And my father was to leave England! Henceforth his life would hang on the chances of battle, and I who had during this long time seen him every day, and counted the blessing so little, might hereafter yearn for a sight of his face in vain.

## CHAPTER VIII.

THE bright days dropped into the sea tranquilly, each one dwindling the sands of time that counted our stay at Treganowen. No existence apparently could be more monotonous, more unvaried than mine; but my outer and inner life were at war. My sensitive and imaginative temperament had been fostered to a dangerous height by the loneliness and peculiar circumstances of my childhood at Treval; like the magnetic needle, I trembled at every touch. My nature, if I may so express myself, had *no rind*, hence every breath of feeling influenced me. To those clothed in a thick cuticle it will seem exaggeration to say that I suffered a positive physical pain when I found myself under the influence of hate, malice, or ill-temper; but the less fortunate who have their nerves laid bare to every wind will understand and believe me. To them do I relate the two incidents that marked my last month at Treganowen.

I was sitting by the side of a little arched well in a sequestered part of the grounds, many a shadow flickering over me, and many a leaf crisped and withered by the long drought dropping prematurely at my feet. The blue of the rainless sky, the heat and stillness of the parched earth filled the air with languor and dreaminess, scarcely a rustle disturbed the trees, the very shadows lay hot and still upon the yellowed grass, and the birds in their languid flight paused in mid-air, or drooped their heavy wings and sat songless among the dwindled leaves. Suddenly, in the midst of this silent heat, which quivered around me like viewless tongues of flame, I was conscious of a strange shiver and frightened wish to flee away. A moment more and a footfall came stealthily over the dried grass, rustling the crisped stalks like the hiss of a creeping snake, then the shadow of a man fell over me, and, starting from my sitting posture, I turned and saw the figure of Mr. Winterdale standing in the path.

He held out his hand to me, and tried to smile; but through the whole of my trembling frame I felt his dim, groping hatred, and I shrank up against a tree to protect myself. His hand dropped by his side.

"I am come to wish you good-bye," he said.

I did not answer him. I would have crept into the huge tree if I could for safety, and, with my hand upon the rough bark, I wished it would open, and shut me from his sight.

"I think you will be very happy with

## MILDRED'S WEDDING. 139

my sister," he continued. "She is a good woman, and she *is* a woman, not a shadow impossible to grasp, which may be fiend or angel, one can never tell which."

I knew this was a stab at Miss Mildred, and I tried to speak and defend her, but my trembling lips kept me silent.

"Have you neither a word of farewell nor of thanks?" asked Mr. Winterdale.

"No," said I shortly.

"And why not, Miss Treganowen?"

"You do not like me, Mr. Winterdale." I shivered as I spoke. "I wish you would go away; you hurt me."

His eyes gleamed with a curious satisfaction as he listened to my words, and scanned my bending figure shrinking against the tree.

"Nervous as ever, I perceive," he said. "Do you sleep well at nights now?"

I looked at him slightly astonished at this pretence of solicitude for my health, then I tried to pass up the walk and leave him.

"Stop!" he cried. "You owe me some thanks surely for prevailing on Miss Mildred to place you at Clifton? Still silent? Then perhaps you prefer school and old Miss Priscilla Polwhele to Hubert Spencer?"

Then I remembered that he was Dr. Spencer's uncle, and I came forward timidly and gave him my hand. He took it, and dropped it instantly.

"You are like your father," he said. "And in your creeping, nervous ways you are like Mildred; that comes of living with her."

"Your nephew does not resemble you," I retaliated. "I should never guess you were relations."

"Hubert Spencer is like his mother, all sunshine and bright colour, no dark spot in him. He is a sunny hill without a shade;

I am a sombre valley, all shadow. And yet we agree; his mother puts us in unison."

"I am glad Mrs. Spencer is like her son," I answered.

A shade, a something, I scarcely know what, passed over Mr. Winterdale's face.

"You will not think my sister like Hubert; it is only I who see the mother in the son. Tell me," he added abruptly, "do you mean to go to Treval to wish that masked woman good-bye?"

"Do not call Miss Mildred names to me," I said coldly; "she is my father's friend."

"Just as much as she is your mother's and mine," answered Mr. Winterdale slowly.

"Miss Mildred has never deceived me. Tell her *that* from me when you see her, and add that I will rip open her secrets with her *own weapon*. I hold it in my hand now."

He grasped my shoulder hard as he spoke, and turned my face towards Treganowen.

"Do you see those towers, Esther? Well, never reckon on their being yours. Lucy Polwhele is not the *only* Polwhele, and you will never inherit them while another Polwhele lives, nor while Bernard Winterdale lives to proclaim the truth."

But here he stopped, checked either by his own prudence or by my small deathly white face, which drooped against the rough tree, as, sickened to faintness by this abrupt allusion to Paul Polwhele, I leant against it for support.

"Good-bye, child," growled Mr. Winterdale, in a rough voice which perhaps hid some compunction. "You are a poor little weak creature, and a turn of the scales would overbalance your brain. There's only a hair's breadth between you and madness: that has always been my opinion, though

Hubert Spencer thinks differently. I don't want to be the one to upset your wits altogether, though, as you truly divine, I am not fond of you. I play no part, you see— no one ever does with you—such organizations as yours, peeled to the quick, were never made to be deceived. Miss Mildred has not cheated *you*, has she?"

The blood rushed to my cheeks at this question, and my heart bounded with a loud painful stroke that made me gasp for breath.

"There—your face answers me," said Mr. Winterdale. "Miss Mildred will never pursue her sister's murderer, and you and I guess the *reason why*. Follow the secret to the end, Esther Treganowen, and I shall know it as soon as you, and then you shall help me to put my hand upon the MURDERESS."

He strode away, never turning to look at me, while I sank down upon the scorched grass and sobbed aloud. Every nerve in my body thrilled with pain. To be intimidated, to be spoken to loudly, to have harsh words and threats rung in my ears, hurt me—oh! it hurt me with such sharp pain that it was crime to do it.

I lay on the grass, my face hidden on my arms, heedless of the fierce sun that glared down upon me from an uncovered roof of blue, while the air, sick with heat, pressed heavily on my aching head, and every leaf threaded with the yellow drought as with some quivering pain, trembling in the dry light, and the only sound that broke the languid stillness, coming dimly to my ear at intervals, was the faint splash of a lazy wave as it crept up the beach, or retreated to the sea, shrinking from the hot touch of the bare rocks blistering in the sun.

Thus I lay weeping till the anguish of my rasped nerves was somewhat deadened, and I could bear to recollect Mr. Winterdale's words without feeling a sharp sensation of pain from head to foot.

His allusion to my weakness appalled me. This shrinking secretiveness, these mysterious clouds of thought dimming my brain, or the fervent visions that swept them away, were they, then, all warnings of insanity? My glowing imagination, my intense love of the beautiful, my passionate feelings and lonely fancies, all so many steps to the dreadful precipice which should dash me into madness? I thought of that blank time spent at Treval, and its secret and darkness became terrible to me when threaded by a fear like this.

It was a cruel fear to put into a child's heart, yet Mr. Winterdale scarcely intended cruelty.

I did not know then that every bear thinks any other skin save bear's skin is some slight gossamer worthless for wear, which the first wind will crack and the first sunlight scorch. He only spoke according to his convictions—nothing more.

Perhaps his mention of Paul Polwhele gave me more real terror. If he knew this man lived, how could I be sure others were not aware of the fact also? And how long could I hope my father would be left in his tranquil ignorance of this ruffian's existence and crimes?

And when he heard of both, what then? Would he become the man's accuser regardless of relationship? Would he dig up that buried history of jealousy and murder, and perhaps put his hand again upon Mildred, forgetful that his own father was not sinless?

Admiral Treganowen had a brother—Alicia and Mildred were sisters—he ought to be merciful. O let the dead rest, my father! let the bloodstained past lie still!

Lately, by some new instinct born within me, I had begun to divine the passion and power of Mildred's early love for my father; and in the searchings and twinings of this fresh insight I somehow connected this love and Admiral Treganowen's crime with her woes.

"Mine shall never be the hand to hurt her," I said.

But by what miracle had the same suspicion entered Mr. Winterdale's mind that lay hidden, as I thought, from all ken in the recesses of mine?

I have said that slowly, through a long course of reading, of conversation, and of thought, I had come to believe in the *reality* of that figure on the roof. While they fought my impressions with the words "disease," "illusion," I was perplexed, but when Miss Admonitia confessed I had seen a *human being*, she tore down the wall between me and the truth, and my mind strode towards it with giant steps. While she on the one hand cried "Sarah Tregellas," and my father on the other cried "Delusion," I put my hand upon the truth and gripped it.

In the workings of my head upon my bed I grasped that terrible half-human, half-spirit face, and unveiled its secret.

*Miss Mildred held a prisoner at Treval.*

Buried in some recess of that old mansion she confined a living woman; there she hid that dead-white face of the blank wall; there she kept that groping figure of the roof, in some sure prison where no eyes had ever seen her save mine.

Was Miss Admonitia cognisant of this fact? did she consent to this woman's living death?

I answered myself with both yes and no. There was something inexplicable, contradictory in her words and manner, as I remembered them, which forbade my coming to a decision. At all events my mind rejected the idea of her being the active agent in this crime. Miss Mildred was the mainspring that moved all at Treval.

And who was this wretched prisoner, perishing in haggard solitude and gloom, whom she kept beneath her iron hand? I thought of that hand so white and small, and silken to the touch, and I shuddered as I answered.

It was surely Alicia's murderer whom she held thus in the grasp of her terrible vengeance!

Read her letter over again, and see how every word of it justified the suspicion. Justified, do I say? Nay, told the fact in every assertion it made.

On the morning after I had received it from Dr. Spencer's hands I rose at sunrise, that with that clearest hour of all the twenty-four I might examine it, with every help my memory and the narrative of Prudence White could marshal to my aid. Then, amid all that still remained dark, this conviction came out clear, that Miss Mildred knew Paul Polwhele to be innocent, because beneath her own soft, cruel hand, in a prison of her own contriving, she held the real culprit.

I remembered in my wild pursuit of that haggard, deathly figure, I had called out, "Stop! demon! thief! *murderess!*" And I recalled the sudden start, the rustle of amazed and sharp fear, and the rapid bound of this creeping woman as she heard my words.

In the blind agony of my terror I had touched the raw spot, I had probed the truth, and my epithets had doubtless pierced her writhing soul.

Reflecting that she might have called to me for help, had she so willed it, I could not avoid a doubt that this woman might be at Treval by her own consent. Perhaps the choice had been given her: this lonely room, this dungeon in the wall, this grave at Treval, or the chains and darkness of the common prison, and the scaffold in the glare of broad day; and she preferred this hideous life-long imprisonment, this haggard solitude, this living tomb, to death in open shame.

Anything, anything to save her wretched life!

Miss Mildred's motives, too, I fancied I could fathom. But they are too numerous for my pen to touch on; think of them for yourselves. Think of her blighted youth, its love, its anguish, its desolate uncomplaining grief, and say whether through the vista of these aching years we cannot see darkly enough to account for her acceptance of this terrible and loathsome office of gaoler to her sister's murderess. Better keep the shedder of blood here always before her shrinking sight than tear up Alicia's name from its hallowed grave, and perchance— for her death surely hid some great shame

—give her fair honour to be torn into unholy shreds by idle tongues. Would a nature like Mildred's, which had already suffered so much to hide some dishonour, shrink from this additional suffering, which would be too secret for the subtlest rumour to guess at?

I thought not. She was not a woman for the sake, the vulgar sake, of hanging the culprit to rip up her own and her sister's youth to the world, the story of their love, their hate, their jealousy, their cruel quarrels, and, lastly, the terrible accusations under which her own name had fallen in the dust beneath the cruel persecution received from her lover's hand.

In my secret heart I thanked Miss Mildred on my father's behalf she had not done this.

I know not how the murderess had fallen into her hand, but through a long thread of gloomy thought I then unwound her reasons for preferring this secret vengeance of justice to the vengeance of an open court. Perhaps when the guilty woman came crouching to her feet, Alicia had long been dead, her very memory was buried in men's minds, my father was married, and had a little child born unto him, Miss Admonitia and herself were grown old, and their hot grief, their aching pain, were soothed by time. Why might they not pity the shrinking wretch, and say, "There, let us cover up this deed, which touches our family honour, and let us hide this woman and her sin till God takes her."

Thus I imagined Miss Mildred had reasoned, had acted, and I pitied her, I wept for her, and I *hated* her for what she had done. A daily loathing contact with crime, to this she had condemned herself for life! No wonder she fasted and prayed; no wonder her face wore such an unearthly whiteness; no wonder the ring of her voice was desolate as the cry of despair.

Nor was this all. Lurking in the dimmest recess of my mind lay the suspicion that this ghastly prisoner—scarcely human in her woe—might have been some friend, some servant, some pensioner of Miss Mildred's, who had *mis*interpreted her wish, and betrayed the unhappy Alicia, thinking she did her mistress good service. Then, when torturing years had gone by, she might have come, haggard with remorse, to fling herself at Mildred's feet and say—

"I did it—for you I did it. Save me!"

I never doubted that any man or woman might commit even murder for Miss Mildred's sake. The wondrous subduing power of her will, the subtle, strange fascination that conquered all natures brought within the circle of her mysterious influence, I had felt and seen.

And what if she had been consenting in the spirit to this ghastly deed? Not by any word, not by any look, not by any furtive gesture, or veiled shadowy glance even, but merely by harbouring in her hot aching heart the dreadful wish that her sister might die. Could she dare, with such guilt upon her soul, deliver up this fellow-woman to justice?

Generosity, pardon, pity—yes, even her own loathing of the creature—would speak like the voices of conscience demanding compassion for the wretch who had become an outcast, loathsome to the thought for *her*, because she had divined an evil thought of hers.

I had eaten at Mildred's table, and sat at her knee, and therefore this dim suspicion of *consent* was horrible to my heart; but there it crouched, ready to spring into life in a moment. Oh, what a fiery torture, what a burning anguish of retribution the daily sight of this *interpreter* must be to Miss Mildred!

I recalled her wild cry that God had punished the innocent for the guilty, her sudden fall to the floor in the crouching and terrible attitude of that haunting woman; I brought before me her fragile form, her white woe-stricken face, haggard with patient suffering, and I read the burning of her spirit, and the wail of its hopeless cry, in every pale line and hollow of her shadowy, shrinking figure. How could the flesh do aught but waste and quail before the quenchless flame of such an expiation as this?

Now I have given you at last the workings of my own mind respecting this mystery. Not that I at all times deemed the hidden prisoner the veritable murderess, the actual slayer of Alicia, but rather the betrayer and instrument who had compassed her death by other hands.

I turn to Mr. Winterdale. It appeared to me that through the cloud of his gloomy hate for Miss Mildred I saw his dreadful thought looming. He, too, had surely fathomed the mystery at Treval. He, too, suspected the presence of some concealed person, held a prisoner there; but for him this woman was Miss Mildred's *accomplice*. In his thought she was the true criminal, and this forlorn wretch only the hand that directed the weapon. Through her Miss Mildred might have paid the blood-money to the robbers, and to his mind it appeared nothing strange that she should keep her instrument safe in a sure prison, unseen by human eyes. I shuddered as I thought of all that might occur if Mr. Winterdale's dim suspicion—I could see it was but a suspicion—of the presence of some concealed person at Treval should grow into a certainty, and lead him into acts which would rend up our peace like an earthquake.

Looking back into his life, I could see some dogged suspicion of Miss Mildred had haunted all his lonely years at Trevella, and rooted him there, in the fixed resolve to hunt her crime from her heart and from her hearth where she had hid it, and track her down into the hands of justice. I could almost lay my finger on the time when this resolve had grown into rock in his spirit: it was when she so abruptly refused to marry the man for whose sake she had suffered so much. What was the motive that worked with such mighty power in her heart that it made her reject this happiness? Perhaps it was at this time that crouching, creeping horror, who bore the shape of a woman, had fallen into her silken hand, and she could not play two parts—she could not be wife and gaoler.

I cannot tell you why I did not myself suspect Miss Mildred—save that the shadow of the crime may have touched her secret wish—of any participation in the foul murder of her sister, unless it be that I shrank from such a thought as we shrink from some hideous gulf into which we know we shall plunge if we look. There was something in my spirit which rejected all belief in her guilt. And I had faith in my instincts. Mine was one of those rare natures that seem to hang on the confines of the other world, ever hearing footfalls from the unknown, ever placing one hand within the veil that covers the soul, ever trembling on the verge of outer lore beyond human ken, ever searching out the hidden things of the spirit; and this strange nature rejected peremptorily all thought of Miss Mildred's guilt, though it never rejected the cold dislike which crept through every vein whenever I approached her.

My cheek has grown fevered, my hand

trembling, as it has brought before you in these hurried sentences a picture of my mental state as Mr. Winterdale stole away through the gloomy trees, leaving me on the grass by the side of the arched well.

## CHAPTER IX.

Hastily I turn to the other event of which I spoke as marking my last days at Treganowen—an event so little outwardly that it disturbed not a cobweb in the old house, nor stayed a single turn in the household wheel of duties that went grinding on. And yet upon this event my whole life was fastened, by this event my destiny was shaped, my love fixed, my heart healed of a great blow. It was a dream—only a dream; pass it over, unbelievers, and turn to a harder page in this history.

It is no marvel, some will say, that with such a teeming brain as mine I should dream strangely, especially now when Mr. Winterdale's words, my agitated thoughts, and my approaching departure all disturbed my mind. No, it was no marvel I should dream, but when my story is fully developed you will see the marvel is not in the dream, but in the strange disease that brought the truth to me in my sleep, and deprived me of its memory on awaking.

In my dream I was again at Treval, seated in the cedar-tree, watching the sharp shadow in its dreary passage on the blank wall, straight up and straight down—no change in the attitude, no change in the pained look of its terrible face. White, white as snow on a grave, and woful as the grave itself, I saw it stop in its creeping, gliding travels and beckon to me.

"Help!" it said with its pale lips. "Succour me! *You* know me."

"I am going away," I answered, "and there is a great blank between you and me which has swallowed up my knowledge of you."

Then the face looked wistfully upon me, a terrible disappointment and grief in every line, and hiding its woe with thin pale hands, it faded away; but as the wall shut it up, I heard a voice falling on my ear like the murmur of water, and looking down from the cedar-tree I saw the figure of Thomas Flavel, the ghost-layer, standing at its foot.

"When next you go to Treval search in the red room!" he said, pointing solemnly with his hand, as he sank slowly, slowly into thin vapour, and vanished.

Here my dream ended, but I fancied myself awake, listening to the voice, and it was only when this had ceased that I sank down on my pillow and fell into a deep, dead sleep. When I awoke from this in the morning, like the king of old, the vision of the night had departed from me, but, unlike him, no dim recollection of its presence vexed my brain. I did not even know I had had a dream. Only that *lost* feeling—that searching, groping action of the mind which I have spoken of as tormenting me vaguely—was hot upon me to-day, tingling my veins with a restless fever, which sent me wandering from hour to hour, to and fro, through the lonely rooms at Treganowen. Moreover, the old sense of duality, the feeling of holding two distinct individualities, one of which constantly hid from me, evading my grasp like a shadow, when time upon time I thought my hand was upon it, haunted me like an impatient spirit fretting every nerve.

The lost look in my strange eyes this day carried a world of sorrow with it, before which I fled, and searching, searching, searching, I travelled up and down and to and fro through staircase, chambers, and corridor, restless and fevered.

Thus it chanced about noon, when the sun's rays played through my hair in a wavy band of fire, I entered Prudence White's room, the pretty blue cool chamber, that faced the west. She glanced at me with a scared look.

"What is the matter, Miss Esther?"

"I don't know, Prudence," said I wearily; "I am haunted, I believe."

Prudence sighed heavily. There was a world of superstition in her that only wanted a breath like this to fan it into life.

"It's a pity some good man can't lay Miss Lishy Tremaine at rest," she said. "Her spirit, or your thought of it, never lets you be. She wants you to do something for her, Miss Esther—what is it?"

"To find her murderer, Prudence; that's what I feel I have to do."

Prudence looked at me with amazed eyes, like one strangely startled by a sudden truth.

"If you feel that, Miss Esther," she said,

"you'll do it. And no matter whether 'tis poor Miss Lishy Tremaine or your own thought that haunts you, you'll be tormented all the same till the task is done. But it's a wisht weird to be laid on one so young. What are you searching for, Miss Esther?"

For I had risen again, and was wandering away.

"I don't know, Prudence, but I wish some one would help me."

"Shall I send round to Trevalla Churchtown for Dr. Spencer, Miss Esther?"

As she spoke a low sob from a distant corner of the room startled me, and turning round I saw Jenifer curled up on the memorable many-caped coat fast asleep. Her flushed face, her swollen eyes, and subsiding sobs told me she had fallen into slumber after a violent fit of crying. Amazed, I looked to Prudence for an explanation.

"Well, Miss Esther, the fact is Jenifer and I have had a quarrel."

Prudence seemed unwilling to say more, but I pressed her so hard that she yielded.

"Where are your keys, Miss Esther?"

"In my pocket, Prudence, I suppose."

"No, Miss Esther, they are in mine. There, take them, and look after them better, miss. For I quarrelled with Jenifer because I found her—the great gawk!—spoiling the lock of your desk, trying with every key on the bunch, except the right one, to open it."

"Trying to open my desk, Prudence?"

"Iss, fye, miss, she were. She said she only wanted a bit of white paper to put round your candle, and she was sure you wouldn't be angry, but when I threatened to turn her right out of the house, and tell you the reason why afterwards, she cried like a child, and then I gave in."

"Poor Jenifer!" said I. "Doubtless

that was the truth. She can't read writing, and I have nothing in my desk but letters from India; she could not want them."

"Have you no money or trinket, miss?"

"Oh, Prudence, don't say such cruel things!" I exclaimed.

"Why, I don't know, Miss Esther, about that. I have not forgot your ma's bracelet. I know she lost it, for all her denial, for Dominy Chitty confessed as much to me. And Jenifer is a new maid; I only took her four years ago when old Tamson died."

"Hush! she'll hear you."

"No, she's sleeping as hard as if she'd been trapesing the house all night, instead of lying in her bed. Besides, she's bedoled with crying, and I gave her a cup of elder tea when I see'd the shape she was in with yewling; so she won't wake up this pure spell. Do 'ee go and look in your desk, Miss Esther, just to satisfy me like."

"But you say Jenifer didn't open it."

"Never mind, do look, Miss Esther; do 'ee now, co!"

No Cornish person resists that little word "co." What it means or whence it comes I cannot tell. I am inclined to revere it as the last living word of the great Trojan or Phœnician tongues, or, maybe, as the diminutive of Corinæus, our mighty founder, whose name, perchance, got to be used as a spell or watchword among the Cornish, till at last, its great potency being acknowledged by "One and All,"* pleaders, beggars, and coaxers have learned to come down upon us with the irresistible monosyllable, and conquer.

Learned men, in arguments quite conclusive to themselves, have traced words back to less satisfactory sources; and at all events, leaving the origin of "co" still

* The motto of the Cornish arms.

in doubt, it vanquished as it always does, and, no longer resisting Prudence's wish, I went to my own room, jingling my keys, half vexed with her, and sorry for poor Jenifer.

On opening my desk, however, I started; it was all in disorder, and a sheet of letter-paper lay on it spread open. I turned it over, and there, in a firm hand not unlike my own, save that I wrote like a child, and this was a free, womanly hand, I read these words:—

"*When I go to Treval I must search the red room.*"

A faint sickness seized me by my heart as I read, for the words, like a flash of lightning, illumined my closed brain, and— I can't say I remembered—no—I *saw* my dream and *heard* it. The deep sleep also into which I sank afterwards I recollected, but I could in no way account for the writing.

After many minutes of alarm and subsequent thought I decided, as the shy secretiveness of my nature prompted, to say nothing to Prudence or my father, either respecting my dream or this strange paper in my desk. I shrank from the coil of surmises it would wrap about me, and I shrank also from flinging any new excitement into my father's mind, darkened as it already was by superstitious fancies regarding Alicia. As for myself, after the first shock the mystery ceased to terrify me; it only stirred me to a more fevered impatience and fiercer longing for that search at Treval on which all the energies of my mind were bent. I resolved on making an effort to get beneath Miss Mildred's roof at once.

If my purpose was unchildish or evil, I was not aware of it. I did not wish to search out that sad, shadowy woman's terrible secret in order to work her harm, but only because this gnawing desire at my heart to grapple with the mystery was fretting my brain like a fire.

Like a hunter tracking down his prey, unconscious of his cruelty, feeling only the glow of pursuit, so did I self-deceptively pen these few lines:—

"My Dear Miss Mildred,—I should like to wish you good-bye before I go to Clifton. Please let me come to Treval for two or three days. I have seen Mr. Winterdale; he was not kind. He gave me a message for you.

"Yours affectionately,

"Esther Mildred Treganowen."

It is with shame I tell of the letter, and acknowledge the thought with which I folded it up.

"If she is afraid of Mr. Winterdale," said I, "and it seems she is—else why had he power to change her determination respecting me?—she will let me come to Treval."

I was mistaken. By the same messenger who took my letter I had a reply from Miss Admonitia.

Treval was full of painters and masons; there was no room in which I could sleep. If I would ride on horseback the next day to Trevalla Cross, she and Miss Mildred would meet me in the carriage, and say farewell.

Disappointed and musing, I determined to go.

I briefly told Prudence there was nothing missing from my desk. Then in the evening I spoke to Jenifer carelessly, confessing all Mrs. White had said. I was fully prepared for a burst of passion or a heavy fire of abuse against the housekeeper, but, to my surprise, Jenifer only rubbed her impertinent little nose and cried again.

"I know I was wrong, miss," she said, "but I only wanted a bit of white paper out of your desk."

"Why did you not ask me, Jenifer?"

Jenifer was silent, save for a loud sob, which went to my heart.

"Jenifer, you cannot write, can you?"

"No, miss."

"You have not left my keys about, so that any one could open my desk and—and play me any trick?"

"No one ever touched your keys but me—oh, Miss Esther, I'm so afraid of yer to-night!" cried Jenifer, interrupting herself in a scared voice.

"That comes of doing wrong," said I, in a highly-didactic tone. "You were never afraid of me before you stole my keys."

"Miss Esther," said Jenifer, looking at me with a white face, "why didn't the doctor come to-day?—of all days in the year, why didn't he come to-day?"

"He had business elsewhere, Jenifer, I suppose," I answered, laughing. "Do you want to make a father confessor of him, and whisper your sins in his ear?"

"I should feel like a hunderd-pound weight off my back ef I could," said Jenifer.

I dismissed her gaily, but, left alone, I thought of that strange written sentence in my desk in a curious, awed way.

My dream did not affect me so much; I read in it only a repetition of my waking thoughts, and there was nothing very singular in my sleeping brain mingling the figure of old Thomas Flavel with a vision of that sad face at Treval. Again I debated whether I would show the paper to any one or not, but turning the subject on every side in my mind, I saw this must necessarily lead to a recital of my dream, and that would so completely betray my peculiar phase of feeling and dreadful suspicion, that it might defeat my determined purpose by arousing Mildred's vigilance; for I felt sure if my father read my ghastly thought, his horror and amazement would be too great to permit him to be silent. Why should I disturb his tranquillity? The time was not yet ripe for making him a sharer in the hideous suspicion that had groped through every avenue in my mind till it reached the centre, and sat there, a firm conviction, directing every concentrated purpose of my heart. I resolved on silence till ripeness was come, and I could show him facts, not fancies.

I might have spoken to Dr. Spencer, but he was Mr. Winterdale's nephew, and this consideration held me back. With that clear instinct which, like a magnetic current, rushed to the true pole of his feelings and purpose, I divined that Mr. Winterdale would make an instrument of me if he could to drag forth Miss Mildred's secret, and setting myself in array against him,

I resolved I would never be a tool of his.

"Dr. Spencer would tell him," I said. And a feeling of bitter disappointment and pain came over me, like that felt by a traveller who sees a great gulf opened where he had hoped to find a bridge.

I slept at last, and my sleep was dreamless.

## CHAPTER X.

To my surprise Dr. Spencer came early the next morning, and volunteered to ride with me to Trevalla Cross. My father seemed glad that I had of my own accord written to Miss Mildred and asked for a farewell word.

"I should be so grateful if you could really like her, Esther," he said at breakfast. "It would be a comfort to me to give her your love. I blighted her whole life. I brought an ill name upon her. I doubt if she ever had an offer of marriage after that terrible event in her family."

The idea of Miss Mildred's marrying struck me as a strange impossibility, and even my father's speaking of it jarred against my nerves. I saw he could never have understood her—never have realised the stength of her attachment to himself.

Dr. Spencer and I had not long to wait at the ancient cross of Trevalla before we saw the old lumbering carriage which belonged to the sisters making its way heavily up the road.

I bent forward eagerly on my horse to catch the first glimpse of Miss Mildred. It was now the end of September, and I had not seen her since November. True, there was the blank time passed at Treval, but I could not bring her face across that chasm; it was only visible to my senses as I had known it before my illness, nearly a year ago. And it was with no childish, uncomprehending eyes I was to gaze at her now. The shrinking dread of my infancy had shaped itself into a reasonable fear, and the blind repugnance had grown to a wakeful pity. I was to look now on her face believing I knew her secret, and could read her terrible penance in every pallid line. I could imagine all the anguish of her remorse, and the exaggerated feeling of fellow-guilt which crushed her day by day, as—even in her utmost pain dealing gently with the wretched prisoner at Treval—she held her securely, bearing her dreadful presence and pouring out her burden only to God.

Thus thinking, I looked upon Miss Mildred's delicate face leaning against the crimson cushions—that face whitened even to deathliness by the contrast, and I met the gaze of her dark eyes with a start.

Why do people seem changed to us if we have not seen them for never so short a time? Why does it take hours, perhaps days, to bring back the old familiar look to the face, the familiar touch to the hand?

Miss Mildred was changed. There was some spirit gone out of her which used to shine forth from her deep eyes in the old days when she looked at me. Time was when, if I had shrunk from her, she too had been repelled by me. That she should repel—the gaoler—was no marvel, but that a child could inspire aversion was strange. Well, this silent, slow hatred was gone; it was interest, affection, that flushed her pale beautiful face as she leant forward, and there was a restless eagerness in her way of welcoming me which formed a marked contrast to the old calm manner, so cold and repellent, which had so often chilled my young veins.

I feared at first that Dr. Spencer's presence would hinder all free speech between us, but she alighted from the carriage and walked up the road by the side of my horse, while the doctor, standing with his bridle flung over his arm, remained with Miss Admonitia.

"You have something to tell me,

Esther," said Mildred, in her soft sad voice.

How curiously that old silvery tone thrilled over me, bringing back in a rush of memory all my childhood—my last morning at Treval—my visit to her room—my terror on the roof—and all the links that brought me here face to face with her, I more a sealed book to her than she to me!

There was an indescribable pathos and anguish in her voice that forced me, in spite of the shudder that ran through me, to answer kindly.

"Her enemy shall not find her through me," I thought.

"Mr. Winterdale," said I, "met me yesterday in the grounds at Treganowen; he bade me tell you that you had *never* deceived him, and he would rip open the truth with your own weapon."

The thin white hand resting on the pommel of my saddle grasped it nervously, but this was the only sign of emotion Mildred gave.

"He hates me," she said. "Was he not cruel enough the other day? What need to send such a message by the lips of a child —a child I love? You do not believe anything against me, do you, Esther?"

I was silent.

"I know," she said—and the old desolate tone rang mournfully through her voice— "I know Prudence White has told you the history your father shrank from uttering, but I cannot think she said anything unkindly of me."

"She never has," I answered.

"Then is it Mr. Winterdale's foul accusations you heed? He hates me—he has always hated me. He has never ceased to suspect me of the most hideous crimes. For him it was I who procured my sister's abduction, and kept her a prisoner among bandits; for him it was my hand poniarded the poor corpse brought to the north porch. Esther, I am growing weary of my life. Your father, and now you too—must I give so much love, and receive only hate? Bid Mr. Winterdale do his worst—what can it matter to *me*? Stop! I will tell his nephew myself."

She spoke hurriedly, a bright flush burning on her cheek, and turning, she beckoned to Dr. Spencer, who came towards us at once.

"Dr. Spencer," she said, "I speak to you because, as Mr. Winterdale's nephew, I presume you know something of his mind, and also because, as his nephew, you cannot be interested in the matter at issue between us, which touches the honour of two ancient families in no way connected with either of you. Being without his early prejudices, you will be impartial; you will see the cruelty of disturbing the peace of two houses for a chimera—you will see the selfishness;

shame and dishonour poured on the head of a Tremaine or a Treganowen would leave a Spencer and a Winterdale unscathed. Oh! if such a stain came near his own blood I might hope for mercy! But do not think I am pleading with you! No! Tell him from me to do his worst, but tell him also he will defeat his own purpose; he will ruin Colonel Treganowen's happiness without finding what he seeks. The sole good that will result from his revenge will be my death. Cannot he wait for that a little while? Great Heaven! have not I waited for revenge?"

She paused, clasping her thin hands together tightly, while the sad music of her voice lingered in the ear like an echo from a cave.

The embarrassment and pain that agitated Dr. Spencer's face astonished me. He had not time to rally and reply to her ere she spoke again.

"I find Esther changed towards me," she said, laying her little hand on mine, and then instantly removing it with a touching pathos and knowledge of my dislike that brought a pang to my heart; "and I have to thank your uncle for this. He sends me a message, too—a threatening message—by this child's lips. Well, tell him I am weary of my life; he will know what that means."

"Believe me, Miss Mildred," said Dr. Spencer, with quivering lips, "I know nothing of any message sent through Esther. You must forgive my uncle; what he feels regarding your poor murdered sister has become a monomania. I am myself obliged to humour him, and he often sets me tasks, or wrings from me promises which I find it hard, and, indeed, in some cases impossible, to keep." (Here certainly the doctor's glance fell on me.) I will tell him what you say, but I beg of you, Miss Mildred, not to notice his madness."

Miss Mildred smiled mournfully.

"It is easy to bear with him while he only treats me rudely or with hatred," she said, "but I tell you the weary truth when I say any attempt on his part to bring my unhappy sister's story again before the world would kill me."

"He cannot mean it; he does not intend so useless a cruelty," cried Dr. Spencer.

"What else does his threat signify?" asked Miss Mildred. "I do not ask his mercy," she continued, as she shuddered visibly, "for myself, but for my sister Alicia. If she could speak to him she would say, 'Let me rest, let the grave hide me, let death pitifully cover my sorrows and my secret.' It is a rash hand that would disturb the dead, Dr. Spencer, and a cruel hand that would unveil the festering pain in the hearts of two lonely sisters."

In talking we had walked back towards the carriage, and as we came within the servants' hearing we all sank into silence. Nevertheless, Miss Admonitia's quick eye caught the deeper shadow on Mildred's face. She put out her hand and touched her. There was a world of love, of desolate love, in the action; it told how these two had stood together against fate, and time, and calumny, and in the unnatural stillness of their lives, empty of all joy, dry and barren as the wilderness, they had yet kept their souls as a watered garden in which to nurture that one holy plant, sisterly love.

Quick to sympathise as a musical chord, quick to see as a ray of light, Dr. Spencer divined my thoughts, and turned a pitying glance on the two lonely women whose cold, proud faces seemed so defiant of the world, so undesirous of mercy.

With a gentle hand he placed Miss Mildred in the carriage, the aid he gave having a tenderness in its touch that came from the heart. The unaccustomed kindness covered her like a shower of warm light from Pity's wing. Distrust, veiled hatred, and suspicion, these had been her atmosphere so long that this unwonted glow disturbed her spirit; she looked up wonderingly, scanning our faces with a desolate look of pain—a pain that told of such long years of hate and anguish that tears gathered in my eyes as I met it. To my surprise, answering tears came to hers, and a softer sorrow than I had ever seen yet shadowed her pale face. Miss Admonitia gazed at her amazed, and would have spoken, but she put up her hand to stop her.

"Admonitia, Mr. Winterdale threatens me, and perhaps I shall have again to pass through the anguish and shame I bore five-and-twenty years ago."

"It is impossible!" cried her sister, with flashing eyes.

"Nothing is impossible to a blind love

and a blind hate like Mr. Winterdale's," said Mildred, "fiercer as both are for being smothered so long. But, Dr. Spencer, *you* are surely my friend and Esther's———"

She stopped suddenly, gazing at me with the strangest look; then in a low, concentrated voice, she burst out—

"Oh! stop him!—stop him, Dr. Spencer! I feel 'tis you alone who have the power to stay his hand. Believe me, he does not know what he is doing. Alicia! oh, my poor sister, will they never let you rest? Shall the sorrow of twenty-five years avail us nothing?"

Her brow contracted as with a spasm of pain, and, shuddering, she covered her face with her hands.

"The honour of our family———" began Admonitia with trembling lips; but she turned sharply from her quailing tone, and gathered herself up in full pride. "Who or what is Mr. Winterdale that he should presume to meddle with our affairs?"

Dr. Spencer made no reply to this; he laid his hand with gentle kindness on Mildred's.

"Rely on me," he said, in a firm tone. "I promise you my uncle shall not disturb your peace. He can do nothing without me."

Dr. Spencer glanced at me as he spoke with a look which I could not understand, but which I long remembered.

"This dreadful story was laid at rest long ago in your sister's grave," he continued, in a tone of deep commiseration, "and it would be cruel in a stranger to drag it forth again. *Nothing* could justify such conduct, except the discovery of the murderer and bringing him to justice."

I felt myself turn deadly pale, and, in spite of all my efforts to resist the attraction, my eyes fixed themselves on Miss

Mildred's face. Her features wore the hue of marble, and a haggardness and horror gleamed through them which she strove vainly to cover with her small white hand. Still, she spoke instantly, and her clear, sad tones shook with but a slight tremor.

"After so many years, Dr. Spencer, there is slight hope of that. God's justice has doubtless long overtaken the slayer of that innocent girl."

As if by common consent, no one replied, and a momentary silence fell over us, during which I felt Dr. Spencer's gaze resting on me anxiously.

"Esther is pale and tired," he said. "Had we not better say good-bye?"

"Yes, I think so, for Mildred's sake as well," answered Miss Admonitia, whose proud face had seemed to utter a silent protest throughout against the whole conversation.

Trembling slightly, I brought my horse to the carriage-door, and gave my hand to the sisters. Both rose, and, as I stooped forward, kissed me.

I could scarcely bear this kiss; something either in myself or in them made me recoil from it. I felt as if the atmosphere of a dungeon were in its touch, the clank of a chain in its sound. Either they or I was treacherous.

"Why do they lie?" I thought, passionately, "and how dare they keep that fearful woman beneath their roof?"

"You will be very happy with Mrs. Spencer, Esther, and, I hope, stronger. You must write often."

I did not hear what Miss Admonitia was saying; the doctor answered for me—

"Yes, I promise Esther shall write often. I have no anxiety for her health; I anticipate the happiest results from giving her so merry a companion as Miss Weston."

Miss Admonitia smiled kindly.

"I shall be glad for Esther to like her," she said.

I looked up, and caught Miss Mildred's gaze fixed earnestly on me. There was a gleam in her eyes that shot a cold fear into my heart.

"Surely she *is* a revengeful woman," I thought.

"This companion, Esther," she said, "will only be a cold stranger to you. You do not care for her, I see."

I answered faintly "No," and turned my horse wildly into the hedge.

Dr. Spencer beckoned to the servants, who during our conversation had stood at a distance — the coachmen at the horses' heads — they mounted the box, and in a moment the carriage was gone.

I looked after it with a hard, unchildish gaze. I felt as though I could crush those two women with a word. The fascination of her presence gone, my compassion for Mildred died away. Her white hand waving from the carriage window shone red as blood against the sunny sky. For a few awful moments I believed her guilty, and during that little space of time I felt a greater horror and hatred for them both than had ever yet steeped my soul in bitterness. Pressing my lips close together, I thought how hard it was that all childhood, all innocent, quiet thought should be wrung out of my heart by my knowledge of their cruel secret. What had their cold guardianship of my simple years forced upon me? Premature reflection, isolation, disease, terror; and these had destroyed my infancy, stroke upon stroke, till childhood died, and a withered woman rose in its place, unnatural, stunted, sickly in mind and body.

O Love! where thou art not there is a wilderness, and in this wilderness I had lived, and grown to this distorted shape.

Cursed was that day when my child-heart sank down into silence beneath the cold roof of Treval. Admonitia might soften to me now, Mildred might even love me—what then? Would that do away with the hate that had crushed my infancy? My nature was formed now; habit is as a strong chain binding us firmly to old custom. I could not unlock my closed spirit with speech; it held its secrets hotly, fiercely, in the clutch of a grim silence, that, like an iron door, shut me up in solitude, barring out my friends.

"Esther," said the clear voice of Dr. Spencer, startling my ear by a cadence of music that struck straight on the sick chord—"Esther, my foolish uncle has built up a wall, a prison grating between you and me, and you will not so much as put one of your fingers between the bars. My poor child, I will not ask you now. Time will bring confidence. I must be your friend, or I wield the healing wand in vain. No matter, Esther, whose hands built up the wall around you: I will tear it down yet, and set you free. Let philosophers preach as they may, silence is disease, speech is health. The babbling brook that runs on whispering to the leaves and shadows is limpid and full of life; fish, bird, insect rejoice in it, childhood plays with it, youth murmurs love by it, and old age grows warm again in its sheen.

"The silent, solitary pool, Esther, lies stagnant; all life shuns it, save the ill life of weed or reptile. No laughter of children, no talk of youth and maiden ever make it glad, no stray foot lingers near it lovingly; hated alike in the sunshine or the shade, it withers, it dwindles, it dries up, it dies, never having given or received a blessing.

"My poor child, my birdie, my little

foundling—for when have you had a mother or a home?—let me save you from this fate."

He took my hand, and bent towards me, the light from his deep eyes—clear fountains of truth and goodness—warming my heart with a glow of comfort so dear, that grateful tears swelled up and rained over my cheeks in drops that fell down upon his clasped fingers holding mine. Then when I saw those tears—I who never dreamed before of showing tears to human eyes—a sudden shyness filled my whole being, and instead of unlocking my speech, this soft kindness, this tender tone of his, shut it in with a firmer key. Ten thousand bolts about me could not have made me quieter than this hot flush of shyness did. It was more silent than the hushed solitude, the cold loneliness, the fevered terror of Treval. But it had this difference, that my silence there was ice, and here it seemed a fire.

And I, glowing, quivering, blushing in its flame, fled before it, half in laughter, snatching my hand away, and galloping close to the honeysuckled hedges, shyly bending to the music of my horse's feet.

## CHAPTER XI.

I DEVOTED the few following days to many a word of farewell to the cottagers and servants, and then, with a sort of superstitious tenderness, I visited my favourite haunts in the garden. Lastly, I stood by the old ash-root where I had fallen asleep on that memorable day in my life whence I dated so many new thoughts and feelings. I approached the tree with a deep blush and trembling of my whole frame, and even when quite near I was still afraid to touch it. I put out my hand and drew it back with a start, turning to see if any one were near to observe me. And it was only after many such an attempt that the tips of my fingers ventured to rest lightly for a moment on the bark. Then I turned and fled, stopping with affected carelessness by a hazel-bush, whose nuts, ripe and falling, dropped lazily in the wind's lap. Seeing no one I came back, and with a fluttering heart measured my height against the notch in the bark which represented the stature of Alice. I was far below it still, and the painful hot flush that stained my cheeks brought tears to my eyes as I marked the distance.

A bed of violets grew round the root of this old tree, and kneeling amongst their leaves, flowerless now, I took up a plant, which I carefully placed in a little pot to carry to Clifton with me.

Yet, somehow, on my journey, when I saw Dr. Spencer carefully minding the little flower, always finding a secure corner for it in the chaise, and never forgetting to water it or carry it within doors when we stopped at inns for the night, my heart smote me with a pang like conscious treachery, and I tried many times to take the sole charge of the plant myself. Playfully preventing all care on my part, the doctor would make a merry answer, assuring me the precious Treganowen violet was safe, or the handful of Cornish soil was unspilt by sacrilegious hands. I bore this with blushes, and an irritated, pained patience that fretted me.

Our journey was without incident, though its tediousness would make this generation smile. We posted the whole way, stopping at night at the town on our road. We were to go to Bath first, and spend a few days with my mother, and as we neared this place a slow fever burned through my veins, though I held my peace and hid it bravely. It was night when we arrived, and I felt my breath come and go quickly as we descended from the chaise.

There was no welcome at the door, no welcome in the hall, and as the servant ushered us into the drawing-room, I saw there was no welcome there either. The large room was dark, cold, and tenantless.

"Mrs. Treganowen is gone to a ball at the rooms," said the servant, as he stirred the fire, and sent a heavy puff of smoke into our faces. Then, after lighting the candles he left us, while my father and I looked chilly at each other across the whole length of the handsome, melancholy apartment. Dr. Spencer was not with us; we had left him at his hotel.

"My dear," said my father, a slight tremulousness in his voice, "would you like anything before you go to bed? I shall sit up for your mother."

I saw he desired it, so I rose and kissed him, wishing him good-night with a pitiful tenderness I vainly strove to hide. Tear-blinded I found myself on the staircase, not knowing whither to turn; but in a moment a sharp, thin, foreign voice accosted me.

"Can I make you to see your room, Miss Esther?"

"If you please, Dominica."

Up another flight of stairs, then another, and through a narrow passage into a dingy, ill-shaped room, furnished poorly with painted deal; no curtains at the window, none at the small bed. I took this all in with a glance as Dominica set a chair for me.

"Madame told us mees would be here only one two days, so it was no good to derange nobody, and she said dis room would do."

I made her no answer. Proudly silent, I resolved at all events not to betray my feelings to a person I disliked.

"I go to send Jenifer to the signorina," said Dominica, looking round the room with a sinister smile, and then departing.

The moment she was gone I flung myself on my knees, with my head resting on the rush-bottomed chair, and tried to repress my tears. At Treganowen I had fancied I did not care whether my mother loved me or not, but now I was near her, her bare, cold dislike sent a quiver of pain through my flesh.

I was disturbed in my sad thoughts by the voice of Jenifer, pitched in that tone which showed that her impertinent nose was fast leading her into a quarrel.

"Ef you plase, young man, I should be glad to be tould," said Jenifer, "ef this gashly ould house es tha Tower of Babil, or a shaaft turned oopside down?"

The person she addressed, who, by a certain thumping and clattering on the stairs, was evidently assisting her to carry my trunk, responded in the Somerset dialect, but my unaccustomed ears failed to comprehend a word of his broad Saxon answer.

"Aw, iss sure, et's tha Tower of Babil,"

continued Jenifer; "and thic be waun of they 'confused tongues' the Scripture tells of. Ef you kickey,* young man, like a coult larning grammar, you caent expect to be onderstood by a Christian."

"I zem it *ez* zummut of a zcrambul to git hup yur, as yur zay," bawled the man, stuttering at every word, and elevating a coarse voice to its utmost pitch in order to insure being understood, but vainly, for Jenifer, now at the door, shook her head at him, and pointed to the stairs.

"*I* warn't brought oop in tha Tower of Babil," she said. "I caent understand furrin gibberish of no kinds."

"Anan?" said the man, helplessly.

"A Nan?" repeated Jenifer. "There's no Nan here, chucklehead, and you haven't got no caall, as I see, to caall me out of my naame."

"Anan?" said the man, again.

* Stammer.

"You can go down-stairs, my son, ef you will," said Jenifer, trying not to be exasperated; "maybe Nan es en the kitchen expectin' of 'ee."

"Anan?" exclaimed the bewildered Saxon, scratching his head, and looking with a vacant and witless stare at Jenifer.

It was too much for her temper. She set down the box and dashed at him, rumpling his shock head of red hair with both hands, and pouring into his astonished ears a tirade of choicest Cornish.

"Thee big timnoodle! thee hulking lutterpouch! I'll knack the great dunderhead through the planchen, I will! Sich imperance I never seed in all my born days, not I! Faith and shoar, I'll get thic bufflehead of thine en coose fur a mop, which es aal et's fit for. I'll fix 'un en a shaape as Nan shall know 'un again. A Nan indeed! I'll teach 'ee! Now, gaukum

what arree standing there for, goggling\*
for gapes like a oogly Glassenbury dog?"

The astonished Saxon wrenched his red mop from Jenifer's hands, and relieved himself of a few of the strongest words in his strong dialect; but when he followed this up by a blow—having certainly received provocation—I grew frightened, and screamed loudly for help. Jenifer meanwhile defended herself by a chair, which she caught up in haste, presenting the four legs at the man's countenance whenever he approached too near.

Dominica was the first whom the noise brought to our aid, but she was quickly followed by the other servants, and by my father. The cries, vituperation, and anger were indescribable till he came. Then Jenifer dashed down the chair, and sprang forward. Words fell from her lips like a torrent.

\* Looking like a fool.

"I arn't come aal tha way from Cornwall to be put upon by furriners, to be beat and swore at en a langwidge the screech-owls throwed away as too bad for theirselves; and I arn't a crow to sleep in a chimley-top, in a croom of a room that a mouse couldn't stand on his hind-legs en. No; and what's more, I'll spaak oop for Miss Esther while there's breath in my body, I well; and I say this es no chamber to put an aunly daughter ento; et's a sin and a shame, et es. I'll be bound Crummell's dog, standing there like a snake en flounces, have goet a room fit for a lady; but my young missus —she as es the aunly child her father have goet—may be pitched anywhere, like halvans* thrawed upon a moor. A bed as a hound woudn't shaake hisself in es good enough for her, but ef Crummell's dog esn't sleeping in silk and satin, I'll be cut up in lerrups,† and be peppered and saalted,

* Refuse from a mine.   † Small pieces.

and put en a pie, and what's more, I'll eat et myself, I well. And where's Miss Alice, who was prinkt out like a butterfly in boots the laest time I was here? And wisht I was then, and wisht I am now; but I won't be put upon. And where's her room, that was next Miss Esther's own mamma's? Caen't her aun child have et, I wonder, or es tha oogliest auld garret in this gashly Tower of Babil good enough for your master's child, you imperent Sarasins?"

Jenifer stopped for sheer want of breath, and then I turned and looked at my father. He was deadly pale. Indignant passion quivered on his lips, and flashed in his eyes, and thundered forth in his voice. The servants shrank away before him as he strode forward and confronted Dominica Cetti, whose evil eyes quailed as the full fire of his wrath fell upon her.

"How dare you put Miss Treganowen in

a garret which the meanest of my servants would not occupy?" he demanded, in a tone that rang out through the house like a trumpet.

The woman writhed and cowered, and tried to creep away, like a reptile crawling out of sight, but Jenifer stopped her.

"Begging your pardon, Dominy Chitty, but Crummell's dog can't be let slink ento a gutter-hole just yet."

Meanwhile my father waited for an answer with a countenance so stern that the woman saw there was no escape. She turned at bay.

"I had the orders of my mistress for what I did," she said.

Then, folding her arms, she glanced triumphantly at my father. He grew still more pale, but, though some new emotion shadowed his face, his anger did not abate.

"Take Miss Treganowen's luggage into

Miss Weston's room," he said to the servants.

"My mistress will be very great angry," muttered Dominica, following us furtively as we descended the stairs, my father and I hand-in-hand.

The neat, pretty room to which the housemaid conducted us drew from my lips a cry of pleasure.

"This is your room, Esther," said my father. "I had no idea of your being placed in any other. When you were last here you shared it with—with Miss Weston, my ward, who will be your companion at Mr. Spencer's, and whom I am sure you will love very much."

This was the first time my father had mentioned to me this unknown Alice, and I was struck by something constrained and strange in his tone.

"I'm wisht to worrit you again, sir," said Jenifer, "but I must have a room close to Miss Esther's. I promised the doctor I'd kip by her alwis, and I caen't do that ef I'm put to sleep oop a ladder among the chimley-tops."

My father opened a door leading out of my chamber into a small room.

"This must be your room, Jenifer."

"Excuse me, sir, that is my room," said the Spanish woman in a quick, sharp tone.

"Then remove your things and take another," answered my father.

The woman seemed to grow beside herself with rage at this order, but he did not appear to observe her passion.

"Jenifer, you had better assist her," he said.

But Jenifer had scarcely taken a step towards the door before Dominica sprang on her like a snake, and, writhing round her, clasped her in both arms.

"No one shall enter my room!" she shrieked. "Listen," she said to my father, in a hissing tone. "Persist in giving this *misérable* my chamber and you'll repent it all your life long."

At this moment I saw in the toilet-glass, which was exactly opposite the open door leading into Dominica's room, the shadow of a man. I was standing by the dressing-table, and therefore able to fix my eyes earnestly on the mirror, and in another instant his face came distinctly into the glass, and I saw it was the face of Paul Polwhele.

Nervous, excited, wearied with my long journey, I could not control my terror. I shrieked aloud, and shrank to the floor, covering my eyes with my hand.

Jenifer sprang to my help, while my father pulled at the bell furiously.

"Go and bid my wife come home instantly!" he cried to the frightened servants. "Take the carriage, and bring Dr. Spencer with you to see my daughter.

Poor child!" he continued, bending over me, "I cannot wonder you are ill. Worn out and weary, you needed quiet and a kind welcome—not a painful scene like this."

He lifted me in his arms and placed me on the bed, but my horror of Paul was so great that I was seized with a fit of trembling, while every sound in the house increased my nervous excitement, bringing on convulsive starts and sharp cries of fear completely beyond my control.

"Send for mamma! Is she never coming?" I exclaimed, wildly.

It seemed an age till I heard the carriage roll to the door, and every moment was a long hour, as my mother slowly mounted the stairs, lingering at every step. My father left the room as she entered, whispering to me that he would but speak to the doctor, and come again.

My mother stopped at the door to ask

for her fan; then she removed her cloak, her hood, her gloves; but she came to my bedside at last, and looked down coldly on my pale features, my wild eyes, my convulsed frame, her own beautiful flushed face, her exquisite figure, her rich attire, all forming a perfect contrast with my weird, witch-like looks. With eager hands I clutched her by her soft lace dress, but a spasm running through my nerves at that moment, my stiffened fingers refused their hold, and fell down clenched upon the pillow.

"The child is possessed," said my mother. "I hate fits—they are horrid. It is just like Colonel Treganowen, to drag me away from a place where I was enjoying myself, and bring me here, where I can be of no earthly good, and only get frightened to death. Send for a good strong woman to hold her. What folly to send for me! I wish I hadn't come!"

She turned to go, but I sprang up wildly.

"Oh, mamma, mamma, stop!—I have something to tell you! Send them all away, and let me tell you, or I shall die!"

My mother looked back on me, and stood irresolute. I saw no fear for me would bring her again to my bedside. I must touch herself, or every chord within her would remain dumb to my cry.

"Mamma, I want to tell you about your bracelet—the one you lost."

"The poor child is roadling," said Jenifer, preparing to leave the room at a sign from my mother, who had now seated herself by my pillow.

"Oh, Jenifer!" I shrieked, clasping my hands together, "not in there, not through Dominica's room! go out at the other door."

"She's dwaling, sure enough," whispered

Jenifer pitifully, as she humoured my wish, the other servants following her.

We were alone now, and clasping my hot hands on my mother's soft white arm, I drew her down towards me.

"Mamma," I whispered—and oh! even now, after so many years, I feel in my veins a faint echo of the agonised thrill of fever, the sharp quivering terror that pierced me through as I spoke—"mamma, Paul is *there!*"

I pointed with unsteady hand to Dominica's door, but as I held my arm up it stiffened and grew rigid, the index finger pointing like a finger of stone. My mother, with a white face, tried to strike my arm down, but it resisted her efforts.

"Dominica!" she shrieked.

The woman came instantly, entering from her own room.

"Is this true what she says? Is he here again?"

"It is true," said Dominica, shrugging her shoulders. "I guessed she had seen him. Now, idiot!" she continued, turning fiercely to me, "do you perceive why madame had no desire for your company so near to her? do you perceive why I would not give to that peasant my room?"

I made no answer, and my hand pointed still. My whole frame now seemed growing rigid beneath the hysterical convulsion that shook me. Again my mother struck at my arm, this time almost with cruelty.

"What is to be done?" she cried. "This child is getting worse. I'm positively afraid of her. I won't live in the same house with her. I've told the colonel so already. I can't be driven mad by fear. It's my belief she's bewitched by that old sorceress Mildred. Esther, put down your arm and go to sleep."

"Sleep! sleep!" I moaned uneasily, "I can't sleep. I think I never sleep."

"Do you hear her?" said my mother. "I can't stay in the house if she goes on like this. Do you remember how she wandered about last winter? I thought I should have died the night she came into my room. Esther, put down your arm, unless you want to make me think that old witch Mildred has put a devil into you to torment me."

"Paul! send away Paul! He's a murderer!"

And my eyes wildly distended, followed the direction of my pointing hand, as, in mad terror, I fancied I saw his shadow crossing the doorway. My fear of this man had something in it scarcely justified even by my knowledge of him. I believe now it was a prophetic instinct—a foreboding of future horror.

"Send him away, down by the little staircase," said my mother, hurriedly.

"Do you suppose he'll go without money?" answered Dominica.

My mother looked bewildered: she put her hand to her brow.

"I wish I were dead," she murmured. "I am weary of it all. I played madly to-night, hoping to win something for him; but I lost, and here"—she tossed her purse to her confidante—"that's all I have. Give it to him, and tell him to go to destruction with it, and drag me with him."

She flung herself heavily on the bed, shrinking in her dislike, however, from my touch, while at the same instant the figure of Paul stood in the doorway. A scream would have escaped me but for her hand, which, quick as lightning, pressed my lips.

"Is this the pittance you give a brother?" asked the evil man in a sharp whisper, coming forward with a creeping, hushed step—a step that seemed used to a stealthy, secret tread.

"How dare you say you are my brother? The child——"

"I know who he is," said I wearily. "Let him say it."

But as he approached me I shrank from him with a great horror, while Dominica rushed forward and locked the door that opened on the corridor.

"Lucy," said the man, flinging the purse into her lap, "I'm not to be put off with a beggar's dole like that. Curse you! don't you live warm, and lie soft! don't you eat, drink, and be merry, while you turn me out to the winds?"

"I can't help it," cried my mother. "I've no more. Oh, go away!"

"No more? And look at your diamonds, shining like a devil's sun on your head!"

"As Heaven may help me," said my mother, "they are no diamonds! I've pawned the real ones for you, and these are false, which I have had made to deceive the world and my husband."

"Whew!" whistled Paul Polwhele. "Give me back the purse then, and get me some money in a day or two. Here, Lucy, you and I have seen plenty of misery together; we won't quarrel; give us a kiss, girl."

Weeping, my mother kissed him, her white arm around his wicked neck.

"Now, since you know me, give your uncle a kiss, little one," he said, turning to me. "You don't look as if you'd trouble this world long. Not much like Alice, is she?"

I strove to move my stony hand to push him away, but the rigid muscles still refused to obey my will, and he stooped over me unresisted, while I felt I should certainly die if his lips touched me; but at this instant a step came swiftly along the passage, and a hand tried the door.

"Thank God! that is Dr. Spencer," I cried out, bursting into happy tears.

"Who?" exclaimed Paul Polwhele, in a ghastly whisper, as his evil face became suddenly blanched with fear.

The doctor knocked impatiently at the door.

"Can I come in?" he said.

Paul Polwhele for a moment stood powerless at his voice, my hand pointing at him still.

"You are a murderer!" said I slowly. "Go away!"

"Hasn't Mildred Tremaine confessed yet that I never touched a hair of her sister's head!" he whispered fiercely, stooping over me so low that my mother could not hear his words. "Ask her the secret of the Red Room."

I gasped for breath, and gazed at him like one thunderstruck, but I had no time for speech or question. All his thought now was to escape. He had held my arm down by force as he spoke, but it sprang up again as he released it, and pointed to him to the last as his evil shadow disappeared through the doorway of Dominica's room.

It was not till another door was opened softly, and the sound of a stealthy step beyond had reached my ears, that my mother with an expressive gesture of silence rose and opened to the impatient knocking of Dr. Spencer's hand.

At sight of his face a sudden glow fell over me, a release as from chains gladdened me, and my hand, which had felt the stony death in it, fell down in warm life and love upon his neck, while my sobbing lips kissed his cheek.

Tears started to his eyes as he lavished soothing words and tender caresses over me like refreshing dew, yet in the midst of his soft pity for me, I thought his gaze wandered suspiciously round the room.

"Who has been here, Esther?" he said. "What has frightened you?"

I clung close to him, so close he must have felt the beating of my childish, terror-stricken heart; but I dared not reply to his question.

"How can they answer to themselves," he asked, glancing at my mother's disturbed face, "for terrifying a child whose peculiar temperament exposes her to horrors of the imagination, and terrors of the mind beyond the power of blunter natures to conceive? Fear, hate, and solitude have killed many such children as Esther. You risk her life or her reason, madam. Such an organisation as hers is not fitted to bear dislike, cruelty, or terror."

"Who says she has had to bear either?" asked my mother carelessly. "She has been brought up by Mildred Tremaine;

that accounts to me for her being more like a witch than a child, and it would still account to me, even if she were more horribly supernatural than she is, if that were possible."

So saying, she swept from the room indolently, as if the matter too little concerned her to admit of her accepting any further discussion on it; yet in going her eyes said "Silence" to me as plainly as eyes could speak. It was strange that she —and all who trusted in my secrecy, liking or disliking me—never once suspected I could betray them. Blind, walled up in darkness as their souls might be, they yet saw that.

"Mamma says Miss Mildred has bewitched me," said I, clinging to the doctor, " or else I am possessed."

"Some people," answered the doctor, smiling, "are possessed with a deaf and blind spirit, and it is a pity he is not a dumb one too—he might then do less mischief. But we'll talk of all that tomorrow. Drink this, Esther," he continued, pouring a few drops of dark liquid into a glass of water, "and try to compose yourself."

I did as he desired, while the kindest hand that ever smoothed an aching brow touched mine with gentle, caressing fingers, and tenderly placed my weary head on my pillow. But the nervous excitement from which I had suffered could not so soon be calmed; and although my father had now silently entered the room and sat down by Dr. Spencer's side, and both soothed me with anxious kindness, still I could not sleep. My eyes wandered restlessly, shrinkingly round the room, and convulsive starts still shook my frame.

"She is afraid of that door," whispered the doctor to my father. "Who sleeps there?" he asked softly, glancing towards Dominica's room.

"Crummell's dog," answered Jenifer, who had glided in, and stood at the foot of my bed.

"And who there?" pointing to another door.

Jenifer made a short gulp, as though some word had risen in her throat which she stopped there.

"Mrs. Treganowen," she said, with a snap, shutting up her mouth like a tight purse.

"My poor birdie," said the doctor, "I don't wonder you cannot sleep. You and I, colonel, might slumber soundly with a cross fire of hatred and motherly dislike—I grieve to say it—hissing over our heads, but unsheathed nerves like Esther's have no chance of rest in such a neighbourhood. Cannot we put her in another room?"

How truly the doctor divined my fear of that deadly door!

"I don't know much about this house,"

answered my father, uneasily, and I saw he dreaded some unpleasant scene with my mother. "I found Esther in a room to which she cannot return; it was only a garret."

"Better a garret than this, if it is safe and quiet. Come, Jenifer, let us go on an exploring expedition. Will you give me leave to find a room, colonel?"

The doctor took a light in his hand as he spoke, and, at a sign of acquiescence from my father, rose, followed by Jenifer, who beamed all over with rays like a shining sunflower.

"First we'll look here, Jenifer."

He walked straight into Dominica's room, while I counted his steps by my beating heart.

"Do you want anything?" asked the thin, sharp, foreign voice of my mother's maid.

"Merely to look around me," answered the doctor, coldly.

" Really, sir——"

" Pray, what door is that? Jenifer, hold the candle close and let me see."

" You need not trouble yourself, sare. I have no thieves hid here. That's a door opening on a little stairs."

" So I perceive. And whither do the stairs lead?"

" Into the street, sare, I believe—I don't know—the door at the bottom is nailed by order of madame."

These words were no sooner spoken than, by a slight noise and a chuckle of great satisfaction on the part of Jenifer, I divined the doctor had descended the staircase. I glanced at my father; there was no suspicion, no fear on his face.

" So far from the door being nailed up, I found it partly open," said the voice of the doctor, after a moment's silence. " I have locked it, and shall take the key to your master."

Not a word from Dominica; doubtless her passion was too great.

"You have heard?" said the doctor, entering. "I would advise you to take charge of this key yourself, colonel, till you get the door *walled* up; nailing won't do. I suspected the child was frightened. Some lover, some rascal, some thief, perhaps, connected with that woman, inadvertently betrayed his presence to her. Is it so, Esther?"

It was useless to deny the truth to his clear sense. "I saw a man," I whispered. And I began to tremble again excessively.

"Not a word more, Esther. Don't speak of him—don't think of him."

"I'll speak to my wife," said my father, rising like a man who feels a duty forced on him. "The woman must leave."

The doctor looked pained. "Say nothing to Mrs. Treganowen," he interposed; "she is attached to the woman. Wall up the door

—that will be sufficient. But it is evident the sooner Esther is with my mother the better."

"She shall go to-morrow," replied my father.

The doctor stooped suddenly and kissed me, his eyes shining with an intense delight. Jenifer clapped her hands and laughed.

"Now, Jenifer, we'll find a room for to-night."

When the doctor set about it, the matter no longer seemed difficult; and my father carried me, wrapped in a large shawl, to a pretty chamber on the other side of the house, far away from the dreaded door and the shadow of Paul Polwhele.

## CHAPTER XII.

The next day my mother received me with more than her wonted coldness, disguising less than ever the shuddering dislike, half fear, with which I impressed her. As I sat timidly silent in her room, the sound of masons at work reached us through the open door.

"I hope, miss, you have done mischief enough for one day," said Dominica, in her thin, jerking voice, as she closed the door and left us. I do not further copy her foreign phraseology—it would but embarrass my story.

I turned to my mother imploringly. "I could not help being frightened, mamma.

And—and is it not a good thing that he cannot come any more?"

"There are more ways than one of worrying a hunted dog," said my mother, snappishly. "There is no telling what he will do now, and perhaps I shall be driven to ask Mildred for help, and I had better ask Old Nick at once, I believe."

"Oh, mamma, don't say so! Surely Miss Mildred is not so wicked!"

"I believe — everything — they say — against her," replied my mother, enunciating her words with slow, clear distinctness. "Why does she never dare to touch Paul? You heard what I said, Esther, that day when you were taken ill? Well, it is true." Here she leant towards me, and whispered low. "I was a little child—a very wretched, forlorn child, Esther—and I saw him do it. He didn't mean to kill that unhappy girl, but he struck her a blow in his anger, and she fell dead!"

My mother put her hands over her face, and remained silent some time. It seemed to me that I could *see* the shudder that crept over her, yet, in spite of her genuine horror and her solemn words, I believed the man's denial of the crime, and I believed Miss Mildred's letter.

"For our sakes Miss Mildred may not like to hurt your brother, mamma."

The word "brother" stung me, but I said it.

"Ah! it's like Mildred," said my mother, angrily, "to tell you that secret. The horrible old ogress!—putting the mother in the power of the child!"

"Mamma, you cannot think——" I began.

"Stuff!" said my mother; "you needn't protest. I don't consider you an idiot. You don't wish to have your mother disgraced, and your uncle hanged; that wouldn't add to your happiness, I presume, so I give you credit for sense enough to hold your tongue. You'll be quiet, as much for your own and your father's sake as for mine; only it is not pleasant to *me* your knowing it, and that's why that walking monument told you who Paul was."

"It was Miss Admonitia who told me," said I shortly, feeling it useless to waste words in assurances that I had more generous reasons for keeping this terrible secret than mere selfishness.

My mother rubbed her nose with great irritation, and flung herself on the sofa among a heap of shawls, as usual.

"Poke the fire, child, and don't talk nonsense. Adder or Mildew, what does it matter which old frump it was? There's not much difference between them—one is a death's-head upon a mopstick, and the other is the mopstick without the death's-head, that all. I'll give Mildew credit for that—she has got a head. It mayn't be an agreeable one; it may be like a witch's signpost, which means there's all sorts of devilry within, but it isn't a numskull like her sister's. I believe your father was right enough when he had that shining white viper taken up on suspicion. Ugh! it makes me shudder to think of her! She hated her sister like poison. She would have given all her fortune to have her put out of the way. And I have no doubt in my own mind she did pay pretty heavily to have her carried off that night. What became of the money she drew from her banker's just before the robbery? It was mighty easy to say the burglars took it; it would be just as easy, and a little truer, I expect, to say she gave it to them."

" But, mamma," said I, "if, as you say, you saw the blow struck that killed the unfortunate Miss Alicia, you must surely know, too, with whom she quitted Treval, and whether she went willingly or was taken by force."

My mother raised herself on her elbow to look at me in a surprised way.

"These are just the very two points that I don't know," she said.

"But, mamma, where were you? How came you to see Alicia?" I persisted. "It is horrible to think it, but were you with the robbers?"

I sank my voice to a whisper as I spoke, and gazed at her in shrinking dread.

"Well," exclaimed my mother, "in all my life, Esther, I never saw such a child as you! If I was with the robbers I could not help it, I suppose, any more than you could help sleeping in the garden of our bungalow with a great cobra standing on his tail watching you, a thing which happened when you were about four years old, and I told your father it was quite typical of the guardianship to which he was going to send you in England. And now I think we had better change the subject of our conversation—it is rather a dangerous one to talk about. You know too much already, Esther, and I cannot enlighten you further at present by explaining all the circumstances under which I saw Alicia Tremaine. I was too young to be to blame then for anything occurring around me, and now my only sin is in keeping these things a secret from your father. Esther, you may pity me or not as you choose, but I *dare* not tell him. There isn't too much love between us now, but if there is any creature on earth whom Colonel Treganowen would hate with his whole soul, it would be the sister of the man who killed Alicia. Paul knows his power, and he threatens at times to fly beyond seas, and from his safe asylum confess all to the colonel, and so insure our misery. It is only lately he has told me that the wretched girl whom I saw die was

Alicia, and that fact has hung like a sword over my head ever since. To get at the murderer of the woman he loved, Colonel Treganowen would sacrifice his wife and his children, besides hating us for having any of that man's blood in our veins. Beware, Esther, how you open your lips, for your father would trample on your body and on mine to bring Paul to justice."

I turned pale and shuddered at the picture she drew of the hate and vengeance slumbering in my father's heart, ready to spring into life at a touch. I felt it to be true.

"I'm tired to death with talking," continued my mother, "and I know I had something more to say to you—I can't recollect what. Oh! do you prowl about by night as you used to, like an unhealthy, stalking, staring ghost, frightening one into fits?"

"I never knew I did, mamma," I answered, alarmed by her words. "I am sure I don't do so now."

"Well, I am glad of it, because if you do I wouldn't advise you to share your room with a schoolfellow. You'll turn her brain with your supernatural ghostly ways."

I gazed at my mother in mute surprise and pain.

"There is only one young lady at Mrs. Spencer's, I believe, mamma—a Miss Weston—a ward of yours I think."

To my intense surprise, my mother flung her shawls aside and sprang up from the sofa.

"Do you mean to say you are going to Mrs. Spencer's?" she cried.

"Yes, mamma."

"Then I shall take Alice away! I'm not going to have her frightened to death by a little weird, unearthly thing like you. You can't help it, I suppose, as you were brought up in a vault at Treval, but you are positively terrible. I'd rather live with the witch of Endor than with you."

I tried to keep the tears back that started to my eye, but they fell down drop by drop, while my mother continued, without seeing them—

"This is just what I might expect from Colonel Treganowen — selfishly exposing Alice to your influence, whether I like it or not; but I shall not submit to it—I shall take her away. It must be his doing—that old mummy Mildred would never consent to your being with Alice."

I did not tell her how Mildred's consent had been gained. I did not say, "Who is this Alice, for whom you care more than for your own child?" I folded my hands, and looked at her in hopeless and silent pain. My mother began to pace the room hurriedly.

"Why should I be kept under the thumb

of those skeletons at Treval?" she exclaimed passionately. "Two dried sticks, with no more feeling in them than in a bamboo cane! As to Mildred, she's like a snake in spirits—a white thin viper in a bottle, looking alive when it's dead, with this difference, you feel *she* can come to life if she likes, and strike you with her fangs. Ah! I wish she was bottled up! I'd keep the cork in, I'll be bound."

"I thought she was your friend, mamma," I ventured to say. "You said at Falmouth she had helped you at some sad time of your life."

"You remember everything, you dreadful little pocket-book!" said my mother with great irritability. "That's just it. She did help me, and a pretty price she has had for it! From the first time she laid her cold, sickly, white fingers on me, when have I felt like anything else but a skinned eel? And I don't get used to it like the eels do. But she shall never lay her silken, treacherous touch upon Alice. And you, Esther, how can you like these old witches?" she cried, suddenly breaking off from her soliloquy to address me angrily.

I looked up astonished. It was the first time I had been accused of *liking* them, and, questioning my heart now, it did seem to *me* that a strange tenderness lurked within it for those forlorn weird sisters, mingled, with regard to Miss Mildred, with a distrust and repulsion which I yet felt some feathers' weight in the scale might turn to an overpowering love and reverence.

"Don't deny it," continued my mother. "You like them better than you do me, you unnatural little thing! I know you do!"

Why are egotists so unjust as always to expect from others the love and duty they leave unpaid themselves?

"And you, of all others, Esther, have reason to hate them. The great fortune you inherit—for Treganowen and Treval will both be yours—will not compensate you for what you lose. And that's just the point I'm debating now, whether I'll tell you what your loss is or no. I don't pretend to understand Mildred's schemes, though there can't be anything in her mind sweeter than poison and revenge; but I have no doubt if I were to tell you only one thing, I should overturn them as easily as I kick over this footstool."

My mother upset the stool as she spoke, hurting her foot in doing so, which evidently increased her ill-temper, for she limped to the sofa with tears in her eyes, and spoke with less reticence than ever.

"I am not a deceitful woman, Esther, whatever my bad qualities may be. I permitted you to see very soon that I didn't like you, and I tell you so again now."

A burning flush of pain and anger flashed hot over my face, and my hands, lying on my lap, clasped and unclasped convulsively, but I uttered no word in reply.

"And I'll tell you why," continued my mother. "Colonel Treganowen can't beat me, I suppose, for telling that much. Part of my bargain with that unbottled viper was, that she was to have you to bring up as she chose. Now a mother naturally loves her child; but if I had loved you, she would always have had her soft, silky hand on the sorest spot in my heart, cruelly tormenting it. So, not being an eel, not choosing to be skinned in more places than I could help, I determined in self-defence, *not* to like you. I made that resolve on the day you were born"—here my mother shut her eyes, as if she were remembering some incident vividly —"and I succeeded. If Mildred had whipped you to death as a child, or shut you up in a dark closet every night to make you mad, I should only have laughed at her. Not one strip of skin has she ever peeled off my body through you, Esther. But in another quarter she has me in her power. There she can put her fangs in my heart if she chooses."

I thought my mother alluded to Paul, and the new insight into her feelings that she now gave me brought a sense of pity into my heart for her, perceiving, as I did, that even her want of love to her child was worthy of pity, being, as it were, only an instinct of self-defence, while her love for Paul left her vulnerable. And so I respected the emotion that worked in her lips and paled her face as she spoke. The gnawing root of her agitation, however, whatever it might be, only made her hate me the more.

"You irritate me to death, Esther," she said. "You sit there so calm and cold; you have no more feeling than those old death's-heads at Treval. What do these old maids think a mother is, I wonder, that they play with a mother's heart as they would with a toy? Do you suppose it would have been no pleasure to me, Esther, to like my own child? Is it no loss to you and me, the want of this affection that would have existed if you had belonged to me as Nature intended, and if you had not—worse still—been set up as an instrument to torture and beggar some one whom I can and do love?"

O God! what would I not have given to have fallen back on my mother's neck, and cried out, "O mother, mother! love me a little! only a little! The crumbs that fall from the full feast of your affection for this other give to me, and I in return will pour into your lap the harvest of a full heart!"

But I could not speak. I trembled from head to foot. I burned and shivered in a breath, as the thought struck me that this other was not Paul, but the unknown Alice, whose height I had notched upon the old ash-tree — the Alice whom Stephen had called " little wife "—the Alice Dr. Spencer had praised—the Alice whose pure white bed, like a soft nest, lay so close to my mother's room that her eye fell on it through the open door last in sleeping, first on waking.

I bent my head lower and lower on my hands, and tears fell through the fingers.

"Ah, I'm glad to see you have some feeling," was all my mother said, as, wrapped in her shawls, she looked alternately at the fire and at me.

Apparently she was in deep thought, and I perceived by the earnestness of her gaze that I was the subject of her cogitations; but whatever her hesitation was concerning me, she soon flung it off.

" Would you like a pretty ring, Esther ?" she said, kindly.

"If you gave it to me, mamma." But

a vague uneasiness shook my voice as I spoke.

"I recollect you don't seem to care much for money," observed my mother, thoughtfully. "Bring that inlaid box over here, and choose a ring."

I handed her the box. "Please choose one for me, mamma. I shall like your choice best."

She turned the rings over many times, and, in spite of my shrinking reluctance to observe the fact, I was forced to see the unwilling, lingering touch of her fingers, and the sigh with which she at last handed me the least valuable of the set.

"You may kiss me if you like, Esther," she said.

I kissed her and burst into tears.

"It doesn't give you much pleasure, I perceive, to have a present. I suppose you don't think the ring is good enough for you?"

"Oh, mamma! mamma!" I cried, hastily wiping my misinterpreted tears, "the ring is beautiful."

"Well, put it on. I am glad you are pleased, though crying is an odd way of showing pleasure. Ah! the ring is too large, I see. I never saw such fingers as yours—they are too small to be human. I declare they are like a sick chicken's white claws."

I bore this comparison quietly, hiding my obnoxious hands, and waiting silently for my mother to continue.

"Esther, you are a very odd girl, but you are certainly clever, and I want you to help me in something I have at heart. Alice, you know——"

I started and looked up. "What can I know about Alice, mamma?" I said, impatiently.

"You may know this much, that she shall not stay with you at Mrs. Spencer's.

I am *afraid* to permit you to be together. You'll hurt and terrify Alice—you needn't interrupt, you don't know what I mean—it is enough that I have made up my mind on this point. But how am I to manage it? The colonel is as obstinate as a mule, the doctor is a gate-post, and Mildred a rock; nevertheless, I verily believe you can get your own way with them all if you choose, so you must just say that you won't go to Mrs. Spencer's—that you prefer going to school instead."

I turned pale, and a faint sickness seized my heart. Was this to be my return for all Dr. Spencer's kindness?

"I can't say that, mamma, indeed I cannot."

"So you refuse me after all my kindness?" said my mother, glancing at the ring sparkling on my finger. An inclination to tear it off and fling it on the floor seized me, but I restrained myself.

"Ask me something else, mamma."

"I have nothing else to ask. Alice is all I care for in the world; if you are her companion, you'll make her like yourself, and I'd rather see her die than see her like you."

"I suppressed the low cry that almost burst from my lips, and stood up trembling.

"Mamma, why do you care for Alice Weston so much?"

"*Why* do I care for Alice!—WHY?"— exclaimed my mother, staring at me in an amazed way. But this was only for an instant; the next she had sunk back among her shawls, and, biting her lips, she said angrily—

"What is that to you, Esther? Don't ask questions. Why did I marry Colonel Treganowen to make myself miserable?" she exclaimed, bursting into sudden passion. "So you'll go to Mrs. Spencer's, and in a few days Alice will know all you know about

Paul. She'll learn to hate me—to despise me—she who is so proud of her ancient name, she will think of me only as the sister of a felon! And is that bitterness enough for me? No!—Alice cannot keep a secret; she would not have the facts that you know in her possession a single day without going straight to the colonel, and divulging all; and the result would be strife, hatred, separation, divorce. Your father would quit me for ever—would he live with the sister of Alicia's murderer? And would he withhold his hand from Paul for your sake or for mine? I tell you he would bring my brother to the gallows, if he trod upon our graves to do it."

My mother's passion and terror altered her voice and her face. All beauty died out of it, as, pallid and distorted, her features worked and quivered with fear and anger.

"I should never tell this Alice Weston any of the secrets of my family," said I, in a tone of contempt.

These words maddened my mother. "This Alice Weston!" she repeated, in an accent of indescribable passion. "Is that the way——" But something checked her words, though not her agitation. She started from the sofa and came towards me, her shawls falling on the floor in a rich heap of colour, and taking me by the arms she looked in my face.

"And I repeat to you, Esther Treganowen, that you would tell this Alice Weston everything. Not by day; but a random question from her at night would elicit all. You are two girls; awake you are as secret as the grave; asleep you are open as the day. Now go to Mrs. Spencer's at your peril, ruin your mother, drive Alice into a madhouse, and hang your uncle. You and your father doubtless could still comfort each other. You are capable of going to Paul's execution, and consoling yourselves on your way home with pious reflections. But so help me Heaven!"—and she used here coarse, strong words, such perhaps as she had heard in her youth— "your father shall not hear this from Alice's lips! Go to Mrs. Spencer's, and I swear to you by the fiery blood of all the devils, I will seek him instantly, and tell him everything myself."

Something of the coarse nature of her brother flashed through the mask of her beauty, as my mother's passion burst the threads that the courtesies and gentleness of her later life had wrapped about her, and broke forth in the strong hideousness of this language. I do not think she could have resisted the temptation to give me that furious shake, which seemed nearly to break up my small frame, as she flung me from her. Exhausted and frightened,

I reeled into a chair, while my mother, gathering up her shawls, threw herself on the sofa, and burst into a paroxysm of tears.

It seemed to me that not my face alone but my heart was bloodless, so cold and deathly had her words made me feel. "Mamma," I said, and my voice quivered with a strange anguish, "if it be true that I talk in my sleep, I cannot of course answer for my secrecy. Any precaution I took in locking my door would not seem sufficient to your fears; you would always imagine some slight accident might betray the truth to Miss Weston. I will not go to Mrs. Spencer's."

Some minutes ago I heard the doctor's step in the hall, and I knew he was now in the library with my father; the thought of his gladsome presence there awaiting me, quivered through me like a poisoned arrow, yet I went on in a quieter voice, "I will do this for you, mamma, but I will not keep your ring."

I drew my mother's bribe from my finger, and laid it on the table, then I left the room without another word, and crept down-stairs pale and shivering.

## CHAPTER XIII.

At the library door, with my cold fingers on the lock, I paused a moment ere I gathered courage to turn it, and found myself confronting the genial face and kindly smile of the friend who never failed me. I walked straight up to the young man, and put my hand in his, but I spoke to my father.

"Papa, I am come to say that I cannot go to Mrs. Spencer's. I know I am a strange girl, and you have been indulgent —most indulgent—bear with me now. I cannot go."

The tight clasp in which I held the doctor's hand must have hurt him, and I knew, through the pressure of this clasp, he felt the trembling of my whole frame, but he said nothing, though his earnest gaze seemed riveted on my small white face. The pain, the mystery of my position, the ignorance and bewilderment under which I acted, confused me, and I returned his look in hopeless, helpless sorrow. A little while ago, and I had rejected Alice's companionship in pride, perhaps in hate; now she—or my mother for her—was rejecting mine as terrible and dangerous. Yet this second rejection was to appear to come from me, with all its accompanying ingratitude and its heartless disregard of my father's wishes. No thought of the false light in which I should stand had crossed my mother's mind as she demanded this sacrifice of me. She loved only Alice; my father—God help my jealous heart! I saw it—loved her too, and there was yet another who loved her; still I was not to be angry, I was not to hate; for her sake I was to grieve my father, I was to lose my friend!

In these few ink-words in which I strive to paint a feeble picture of my pain, there lives only a faint image of the strong suffering with which I battled as I spoke the first short sentence to my father. What would I have given to have thrown my arms around his neck, and hide my poor little worn face on his shoulder, that he might read the truth in my tears and the throbbing of my heart, for speech to tell him I had none!

"What is the meaning of this, Esther?" he said, sternly.

My chest heaved, my lips quivered. "I cannot go," I answered.

"This is childish folly—you must go!" he replied, with increased anger. "I quit England in a few days to brave all the chances and hazards of war, to face death in countless ways, and this is the time you choose to fill me with anxiety and pain! How can I leave if you refuse to accept the safe and happy asylum I have secured for you? You are not a child, and I expected sense and kindness from you, Esther."

The pain and disappointment in his tone blinded my eyes with tears. I tried to say again "I cannot go," but I broke down, and only turned a wild look on him, shaking my head as a negative.

"If I lay my commands on you, Esther, you must obey, but I am willing to hear your reasons. Why do you object to Mrs. Spencer's? Is it possible you dislike the doctor? For answer I looked at Hubert Spencer. I looked full into those wonderful eyes that no other face had, or ever could have, and the clasp of my small hand appealed to him with the eloquence of a thousand words, pleading for his help. With what childish love and confidence I looked I never knew till he told me in after years.

"It is not that: she does not dislike me," he said.

At these words I broke from him and ran to my father, and kneeling down by his chair, I clasped his arm, and sobbed speechless. But, angry with my unreasoning disobedience, as he deemed it, he would have raised me sternly, had not the doctor come to my help.

"Leave her alone a little," he said; "she is so troubled she cannot speak. Remember her painfully sensitive nature, and how strangely it has been tried," he added, in a low voice.

At these words my father stooped and kissed me, then I gained courage; I spoke out wildly—

"Oh, papa, take me back to Treval! Let me stay there while you are away! I have read of long-imprisoned captives set free who wept to be taken back to their dungeons. I am like them. I am only fit for Treval. I have been lonely all my life. I could not bear strangers—above all, this girl, Alice Weston. What do I know of girls? I could not endure to be with her—I should be *afraid* of her—I should feel in chains in her presence. I have always been companionless; I want no schoolfellows, no friends, no sisters. Papa, take me back to Treval, where I shall be lonely again; and forgive me, or I shall die."

Some great emotion worked in my father's face as I clung to him, holding his hands pressed against his cheeks, wetting them with tears.

"This is dreadful," he said, as if to himself. "What does it mean?" he added, turning to Dr. Spencer. "She showed no repugnance to our plan at Treganowen, and even so late as yesterday she seemed content and glad."

I dared not follow his glance; I could not look at the face of Dr. Spencer; I was giving up all thoughts of seeing it, perhaps for ever; I was renouncing all my dreams of happiness beneath his roof—all my hope of living my daily life in the " full feast of his presence," as Jenifer had said; I was going back to hunger and emptiness—I was going back to prison at Treval.

" It means," began the doctor, in answer to my father, " that Esther———"

But here he stopped, for I turned suddenly and looked at him, imploring silence by a gesture. In the expression of his eye, in his glance towards my mother's portrait, I read that he had divined a portion of the truth.

" It means," he continued, " that Esther is sensitively nervous to the presence of a stranger. If Miss Weston were not with my mother, would you come?" he asked.

The hope that glowed within me at his words burnt on my face in a blush of fire.

" I would go then," I said softly.

"Colonel Treganowen," said Dr. Spencer, "you must remove Miss Weston from my mother's care. This is a fixed idea on Esther's part, and we must yield to it. All things must yield to her health and happiness. I have set my heart on restoring her to you on your return, blooming in health and beauty. Give me my way. Miss Weston has no need of me. This poor little dove"—he lifted me from my father's feet, and gathered me in his arms—"has been terrified, imprisoned, wounded almost to death. I cannot give her up for twenty such blooming, flourishing flowers as Miss Alice Weston."

My father remained silent. Some deep pain sat upon his face, betraying a strength of sorrow I could not comprehend. Dr. Spencer regarded him with a look of respectful pity.

"It is a disappointment," he said—"a bitter one. I can comprehend all you feel.

A great hope has quitted us both. We cannot help it. A forced companionship would bring none of the results we desire."

"Oh, Esther!" said my father, breaking forth in a cry of sorrow, "you know not what you do! I thought to quit England accompanied by one happy hope; you have killed it. Dr. Spencer, I will remove Alice, but, as you truly say, the disappointment is bitter. I thought to give my poor lonely child a companion. I hoped, in spite of Mildred's long hate, to find her a sister. Oh, Esther, you cannot dream the pain you give me."

With eyes full of pity he looked down upon me, and with eyes full of pity I looked up to him.

"Oh, my father!" I thought, "the pain of knowing that such a man as Paul Polwhele lives would be greater than this pain, so I gather courage to bear your words."

"Delay is useless. I will send the

servants and carriage for Alice at once."

My father turned to leave the room, but, glancing towards my tearful face as I stood trembling with my hand on Dr. Spencer's arm, he came back and kissed me.

"Do not think I am angry, Esther," he said; "the fault of this is not all yours."

"This is your mother's doing," said Dr. Spencer, the moment my father had closed the door.

"Yes," I answered softly.

"Will you tell me her reason?"

"No, never!"

I tightened my clasp on his arm and turned pale at the thought.

"It does not matter—I shall find it out."

## CHAPTER XIV.

It was decided at first that I should depart in the carriage which was going to Clifton to fetch Miss Weston, but as my father wished to show me the city, and make many purchases for me, Dr. Spencer proposed that Jenifer only should go in the chariot, and that I should accompany him in his chaise, and it was thus arranged.

We started late in the afternoon, after a cold farewell from my mother, and many promises from my father to visit me as often as possible before he quitted England. If I felt sad on parting, Dr. Spencer soon beguiled my grief by little rills of talk, and laughter, and song which burst from him naturally, not as if he were pouring them forth to amuse me, but as if he could not help their bubbling up like a spring from the full fountain of his happy nature.

It was the beginning of October; day soon closed around us, and we travelled through a golden sunset into a rosy twilight, through which Night came daintily to meet us, gliding softly beneath her canopy of stars, pressing perfume with her feet from the autumn flowers. At her approach the winds crept into the trees to rest, and the incense-bearing air wrapped us about in hushed darkness like the leaves of a lotus-flower. Gradually silence fell down upon us—a silence dreamy and full, teeming with strange thought—not the shadowy thought of sleep, but visions that drop from the over-brimming cup of young life; these held me as in a spell, while the waving trees in uncertain shape passed by to the music of the horses' feet, and the melody and march of the sounding world as it travels stately through the night lulled me into a pleasant weariness, which stole upon me with a breathlike rest. And the doctor was silent too, holding me like a jewel in the warm ring of his arm, cradling my head on his shoulder; and thus resting, the visions dropped, then started up again, then danced brokenly in the shining shapes that came and went without a meaning, and I slept.

I slept, and yet in another carriage I saw myself sitting alone and sorrowful, only I was taller, fairer, and the glow of health mingled with the glow of light flashing from the lamp on my bright cheeks. But my eyes were wet with tears, and yet they smiled, and the old lost look had faded away, quenched in a sea of love in which they swam. Loose upon my shoulders my hair floated, and the golden wave of fire that rippled through it had died out in ebon blackness. And I was fair, very fair, and beautiful exceedingly, and leaning from the carriage window I put out a timid hand and arm steeped in the moon's rays like a mermaid's rising from a sea of silver, and I sought to touch the unlovely, weird, and solemn Esther, who, pale and sickly, slept on Hubert Spencer's arm.

"Ah, do not envy her her father's heart, she has but him in the world."

The voice came into my dream like his, but I slept on, and my hand—the hand of my other self—stretched far out from the window, and would have touched me on the brow, but another voice silver-clear rippled in upon my sense, and I broke from my sleep with a cry trembling upon my lips—"Stephen!"

Who said it? what was it? I trembled as I asked myself. And in awaking I felt as though some shock had divided me in twain, taking from me that other self for whom such long years I had been dimly seeking. But I was alone with Dr. Spencer, and on one side the road was very dark, but on the other lights gleamed—a carriage was passing by, and for a moment's flash I saw the figure of a fair girl sitting alone, her face hidden in her clasped hands, her hair in a dark shower covering her fair shoulders; then she was gone, and I should have thought the vision still a dream, save that the beat of the horses' hoofs and the rumble of the departing wheels were real sounds.

"Poor Alice!" said Dr. Spencer. "She was weeping; doubtless she is grieved to quit my mother."

And from out of the darkness a voice echoed, clear, and sweet, and sudden, as though a star had spoken, dropping silvery music to our feet.

"Poor Alice! she has wept the whole way." I turned, and on the dark side of the road loomed the figure of a horseman. "Do not be frightened," whispered Dr.

Spencer, as the violent bound of my heart beat against his arm. "It is a friend of mine."

"I know him," I answered. Then I put my hand out and took his. "Thank you for the 'Faerie Queene.' I've read it through and through. You are escorting Alice, the girl you called your little wife; but there is no need; she is quite safe in papa's carriage, with two servants to protect her."

The young man laughed, and the moonlight made his face look pale.

"I am not escorting Alice, Miss Treganowen; I happened to be going this road to-night, that's all. Are the ladies of Treval well?"

"They are well," I answered.

"And you—are you better?"

I felt the tightened clasp of the doctor's arm, but I released myself from it, and leant from the window.

"The carriage is fast disappearing. Had

you not better gallop after it, instead of asking questions to which you scarcely desire an answer?"

"We are friends, I hope?" said Miss Admonitia's godson, riding up quite close, and putting his hand on the window-sill.

I made no reply.

"Ah, I see you are still thirteen hundred years old———"

"No, I am fourteen now; indeed, nearly fifteen———"

"But no younger," broke in the young man, "and as much my enemy as ever. Farewell, fair Capulet. Won't you say adieu?"

"Why adieu?" I asked. And a slight quiver on my lip made me stop short.

"I go to-morrow to Southampton, and thence to Lisbon. My guardian griffins at Treval seem to think a little killing will do me good. I have liberty to risk shooting, drowning, and hanging for three years;

then I return to—to my fate, I suppose," he added, carelessly.

"What can it matter to me where he goes?" I asked myself.

"Well, I'm glad of it," I said.

"Glad for what? That I go to my death, or return to my fate—which?"

"I am glad you go. Thank you again for the 'Faerie Queene.' Good-bye; the carriage is out of sight."

"Your feelings do you credit, Miss Treganowen. Had you shown me the least kindness, I was about in return to promise you that I would get killed if I could, and if not, I would defend your father, and bring him back safe from the tide of war, if friendship and affection can do it."

"Are you going with my father?" I cried.
"If you will indeed try to guard him——"
I stopped, a little confused.

"If I guard him?" repeated Stephen, bending low from his saddle. "Pray finish. I feel like a knight of old, about to be rewarded by some fair queen of beauty."

I knew he was quizzing me, and my face flushed, while Dr. Spencer appeared irritated.

"Excuse me," he said, "I'm going to close this window. When one has charge of an heiress, one must be careful of her health. You know I am guarding here the houses of Treganowen and Treval."

I could not understand the shaft, but it struck home, for the young man's laugh fell suddenly into a blank silence.

"You will find it difficult to overtake Miss Weston now," continued the doctor. "Had you not better make haste?"

"What does it matter about Miss Weston? She is not an heiress, you know," answered Stephen, bitterly. "If the coachman tilts her into the hedge, and breaks her neck, half a county will not go into mourning for *her*."

"But that is not the case here," observed the doctor in his blandest manner, "so pray permit me to put up the window."

His hand was on it, when Stephen stopped him in a polite but cold tone.

"One moment, I beg. Miss Treganowen, pray shake hands with me, and say goodbye. You may wish a shot may reach me if you like. I don't much care. I am a sad, reckless dog, and good for nothing else but food for powder. When you write to Miss Mildred, you will not tell her we met as enemies?"

"I have never mentioned you to Miss Mildred, and it is not likely I ever shall," I answered.

"Oh, really? Well, I'm glad of it," he said, in a relieved tone. I fear you would not paint me in *couleur de rose*, and you know I have a wholesome fear of Miss Mildred, and don't wish to offend her."

During this speech he bent forward, and

seemed to be endeavouring to look at me, but I held my face out of the moonlight and disappointed him.

"If you fear our meeting as enemies would offend her, you can put your mind at ease. I have no enmity or any other feeling regarding you that I am aware of, except being much obliged to you for the book."

An expression, half vexed, half amused, passed over his face.

"Old as ever," he said.

"Older," I answered.

"And in all else unchanged, I presume?" he returned, trying again to peer into my face. The slight sarcasm in his tone cut the reins of my temper.

"I am quite as plain as ever, and as steadfast as ever in my likes and dislikes, and in resistance to all tyranny, present and future. The carriage is out of sight, and papa's horses are good; you have lost all chance of overtaking Miss Weston."

I leant back on my seat with the air of a person who intends to say nothing more, and again Dr. Spencer would have closed the window, but Stephen's hand interposed. He held it out towards me, and my fingers were clasped within it, with scarcely a consciousness on my part that I was obeying his wish.

"Without malice, Miss Treganowen?" he asked.

"Certainly," I faltered, as, hiding in shadow, I glanced at his handsome face, shining in the moonlight.

"Let us say good-bye kindly," he continued. "No need to torment each other now. We shall have time enough for that in our future lives. You are only a child— you cannot understand how some things may make a man fume and fret, and show himself different to what he is." He wrung my hand, took off his hat to Dr. Spencer, and galloped away. The window remained open, and though I shivered perceptibly, my companion for a moment took no notice; then he closed it hastily.

"Esther, you took too much trouble to show Sir Stephen Tremaine you do not like him."

"Is that his name?" said I, evading a reply to this remark.

"Is it possible you did not know his name?" exclaimed the doctor.

"How should I? Have I not been brought up as a prisoner, through whose dungeon-doors no intelligence was ever permitted to penetrate? Who is Sir Stephen Tremaine?"

"I suppose I interfere with no family arrangements by giving you that simple information," said Dr. Spencer. "He is a distant relation of the Misses Tremaine, through the sister of the first baronet, who made a runaway match, and was ever after repudiated by his family. However, on the death of Sir Theobald, his daughters sought out their cousin, who was living in great obscurity and poverty with his widowed mother at Bristol, and charged themselves with his education. And just before you came from India, Esther, they, conjointly with this lady, petitioned the crown that the baronetcy—extinct or dormant by their father's death—might be conferred on him. The county of Cornwall, you know, returns as many members, within two, as the whole kingdom of Scotland,* and so many boroughs are in the Misses Tremaine's hands, that no request of theirs was likely to be refused. Their young relative, Stephen Carpenter, had the baronetcy, and took the name of Tremaine; they make him a handsome allowance, for he is quite dependent on them, and they give him

* A fact at that period.

every reason to suppose that at their death they will leave him ample means to keep up the rank they have procured him. Whether they annex any price to their gifts, Esther, I scarcely know, though by his irritable manner I sometimes fancy they do. His mother, to whom they gave a liberal annuity, is dead. These are facts every one knows, and I see no reason for secrecy, else I would not tell you."

I perceived the agreeable matrimonial arrangement which Stephen had betrayed to me was unknown to the doctor, although he might suspect it.

"And do you know Sir Stephen Tremaine very well?" I asked.

"No, I know him but very little. I have lived much abroad, and though on my return home I found him a frequent visitor at my mother's, yet as I went almost immediately to Trevalla, to be near a little patient who interested me, I did not get very intimate with Sir Stephen Tremaine. He has a house at Clifton, so we should have seen a good deal of him if he had not so suddenly made up his mind to join the army."

"He does not appear to be enthusiastic on the subject of fighting," said I, dryly.

The doctor laughed. "I assure you he was very comfortable at Clifton. He won't find life so easy in Spain. However, I am rather glad he is gone."

"Oh! if he had stayed at Clifton he would not have troubled your house much now Miss Weston has left it."

Dr. Spencer brought my face into the full sheen of the moonlight before he answered me.

"You have come curiously near a thought of my own, Esther," he said. "Miss Weston, although the same age as yourself, is not at all a child in appearance, and she is very beautiful, and I believe very poor. Now I imagine Sir Stephen is not a man who would ruin his prospects for love, and I should be sorry if your mother's ward formed an attachment to him, as I suspect Miss Mildred has schemes of her own respecting his future, on the fulfilment of which will depend his fortune."

My heart swelled within me. I knew the doctor's suspicion was correct, and Stephen Tremaine and I were both disposed of by a cruel family compact. I guessed that without me—whom he hated—he would never possess Treval, and I foresaw that the fear of poverty and habits of luxury to which his cousins' liberality had accustomed him would make him accede to this odious bargain. Tears stood in my eyes as a thousand indignant resolves and plans of resistance passed through my mind, and my spirit rose up in passionate remonstrance against my humiliating position. To be received as a hateful appendage to an estate, to feel that a man was compelled to take me or be ruined, was a bitter thought, and young as I was, I understood the galling pain and shame of such a marriage.

"If Miss Mildred's scheme has to do with me——" I began passionately.

"Hush!" interrupted the doctor. "There are many suns must arise and set before they can speak of such things to you. And how do we know what chance the years may bring? Why, the French may let the troublesome life out of Sir Stephen's well-knit frame before then, or Treganowen Towers may be undermined by a ghost, and you rendered a dowerless bride; he would not prove an importunate suitor in that case."

"You do not like Sir Stephen," I said.

"You are mistaken. He fascinates me, and I like him extremely, only in playing with a strange animal we yet guard against a bite, and there is an instinct in the lowest creature that breathes which tells it when peril is near. If that instinct pricks me sharply in Sir Stephen's presence can I help it? Here are the lights of Bristol."

## CHAPTER XV.

When I saw Mrs. Spencer, I thought of Mr. Winterdale's words, that I should not think the mother much like the son, and I looked in vain for the sunshine and bright warmth of which he had spoken.

Mrs. Spencer was a handsome woman of a portly presence, not without kindliness and geniality, a certain motherliness, as it were, pervading all she did; but the healthy, sound, clear, glad nature of her son, full of summer warmth, had in her stopped short at spring, and she was subject to many little frosts and changes, which nipped the full blow of love in the heart for her. As days glided on, and we quietly sank into a well-ordered household, workful, cheerful, and kindly, I began to study her more earnestly, and my first discovery shocked me a little. I found she loved her brother better than she loved her son. Mr. Winterdale was her idol. He was held up for household worship on all occasions possible, and there was an incense of reverence sprinkled even over her commonest talk when his name slipped into it. The doctor bore this with a good humour all his own, a twinkle sometimes in his grey eyes, or a sly smile curling round his lips, alone betraying that he was aware of his mother's weakness. Nevertheless, I fancied at times that Mr. Winterdale was to him, like Sindbad's old man of the mountain, slightly oppressive, and this not by reason of the too heavy shower of sisterly praise pouring over us from the household eaves, but for some cause known to himself, which shackled not his actions only, but even his free thought. This was my impression, and not being of the logical sex, I never reasoned on it, but waited patiently believing it, till time proved it correct.

There was a good library in the house, and on scanning the books with my usual hungriness of eye, I was amazed to find Mr. Winterdale's name on the title-pages of many—" A Treatise on Runic Inscriptions," "The Footsteps of the Lost Ten Tribes Patiently Tracked," " Druidical Characters Deciphered," " Siftings among the Ancient Phœnician Idolatries."

These and others I took down from their shelves, and looked at with a weary sigh. We may live near a man for years, and yet never see him with understanding eyes. We know no more what is in a man by our conventional acquaintance with him, than we know the caves, the rocks, the springs, the flora, or hidden wealth of a mountain by measuring its shadow. My friends, it takes a long time to *see* a man. Bear this in mind when you meet a poet, a hero, or a worker in the mines of thought, and do not come away disappointed because the shadow you have seen was smooth and ordinary, and perchance of as dull a grey as any other shadow you have jostled in life. Remember it is the shadow, not the man, and reflect also that yours may not be a vision that can see *more* than shadows, so be silent when you step back into nothingness, and neither hiss nor clap—what is your praise and what is your blame to him?

These men, witnesses for truth, whom we call by names that deify—prophet, poet, hero—are simply those whom God has endowed with a greater power to *suffer* than their brethren; and the earth which they too often water with their blood hides their pain and her remorse in monuments and crowns, and cries—Behold their glory!

With feelings of painful insignificance I took down the works of erudite research which Mr. Winterdale had given to the world from his quiet nook at Trevalla. That such a man, hiding all his well won renown from my childish reverence, should have condescended to be my tutor, daily training my mind, as I now tremblingly acknowledged, into the same untiring, tracking, twisting power of research, steeping my spirit in the same patient curiosity that characterized his own, amazed me. Breathlessly I dived into his motive for such a course of conduct, and put my hand on it without shrinking. I observed that every work he had written was a finding out of something hidden, a dragging forth of proofs, a digging up of musty facts, and I felt that he had not cared to know these things for themselves, but had worked to train his mind into a great power for patient investigations, that should never tire or flag. And to this end too he had moulded me, meaning to make me a trenchant weapon in his hand. That I had imbibed this spirit of search, patient, unflagging, that I was soaked through and through with it, I confessed, but that I would let it be turned against Miss Mildred I denied. He forgot that in giving me a spirit like his own he was perhaps only training me to be an equal foe.

I began a course of reading through his laborious works, not to know *them*, but to know *him*. Step by step I followed him through researches so wearisome that I marvelled more and more at the brain which could explore such dry, dusty caverns of thought, and never weary by the way.

Dr. Spencer laughed at my new studies; but as his mother watched me reading, a glow of pride warmed her face, and her admiration for me visibly increased. At first she had been inclined to consider me either incomprehensible or stupid, but seeing me interested in her brother's works, her judgment shifted, and I mounted to the topmost ring of her esteem. Thus I was for a moment surprised when, some time after my arrival at Clifton, she one morning suddenly refused me the key of the bookcase in which these precious volumes were enshrined, telling me with a fixed look that I was to read no more of them. The next instant I had guessed the truth, that it was her brother himself who had given these orders, knowing me better than she did, and mentally wincing at being morally dissected by the girl in whose spirit he had helped to create an artificial imp of curiosity.

Frequent letters passed between Mrs. Spencer and her brother, and I could not help feeling that I was often the subject of their correspondence.

In speaking of Mr. Winterdale I have slightly anticipated my narrative. I go back a little to say that I saw my father three times before he quitted England, that each time he evinced a tenderer solicitude for my happiness, and on parting was full of grief and affection, though neither his speech nor mine touched the topics perplexing our thoughts. He did not mention Stephen's name, and a shyness that was almost pain withheld all questions from my tongue.

My mother did not accompany my father on either occasion, but after his departure she came and graciously thanked me for my obedience to her wishes—" my clever manœuvring " she called it. She told me Alice was at school at Bath; then she whispered that Paul had got into a terrible scrape, and she had had to find money to help him to escape, and he was gone abroad. She seemed relieved at this, and in better spirits than when I had last seen her.

I go back again in my story to say that in Alice's room I found a "Faerie Queene" like mine, but new and unread, and it had her name in it, with "From her dear friend, Stephen Tremaine," written beneath. And many other tokens I found of his thought running through Alice's life like a golden thread. Here were his initials, intertwined with hers, carved on a tree in the garden, and her name was flourishing in a border of mignonette, doubtless sown by his hand. On her window-sill stood some pots of rare flowers, and I needed not the pencilled list behind the shutter, giving the dates of each gift, to know that they came from him. I looked at all these things silently, never asking a question, but finding them out for myself. I slept in Alice's room, and I let the plants in the window die out one by one for want of water. I never took a spray from the mignonette border, and if Dr. Spencer brought me one,

I always asked in a laughing tone where he had gathered it, and if it came from the obnoxious bed I tore it up, or flung it away when I was alone. During the three years I stayed with Mrs. Spencer, I never once touched the tree on which those initials were carved; and when the winter came I stood before the mignonette border, and watched Alice's name shrivelling, dying, perishing, with a superstitious pleasure that ran cruelly through my blood. Avoiding all questions, I nevertheless elicited a thousand particulars from Mrs. Weston respecting Alice. Soon I could read her disposition in all its gaiety, its carelessness, its easy cleverness, its indolent talent, its half selfish, half generous lavishness of love on all around her—a love which she forgot the moment they were gone, but which remained with them like a root of bitterness—and particularly I could see the charm of her presence lingering in the house, and in the hearts of those who had come under her spell. I knew that in her keeping was treasured up all the affection my mother was capable of feeling, and that no word of kindness, no thought of love ever fell to my share. She had stolen all—all. And I knew—only I would not know it, lest I should hate her too madly — that my father cared for her also, but I comforted myself by saying it was but a little, because his tone trembled and his look turned wistfully to me when he spoke her name.

And all things in this house breathed of her—books, birds, music, flowers. Stephen had sown her name in mignonette, and carved it on the tree, and written the list of her plants on the shutters, and measured her height against the wall, and marked the date and her age—the same as mine, but the stature how different!—in pencil, and signed it with his initials. And on the little trellised high window in the summer-house were verses—silly verses praising her beauty—written with a diamond. I laughed at them as I stood on the bench to read them, yet I wetted my pillow with tears that night.

I cannot help it if I hated Alice; the hate grew upon me, and I never knew its intensity till time tried it, and showed it to me in its fruit.

Surely I have spoken enough now of my mind and moods of thought, and you can fancy all that was working within as I carry you on through the outward events of my life.

I was not unmindful of my mother's strange words respecting my troubled sleep. I had a great fear of this, and every night I locked my door carefully, and bolted the door which opened between Jenifer's chamber and mine. I had no mind that even she should hear me rambling of Paul

Polwhele, or of any other secret thought tormenting me.

I heard often from my father and from Miss Admonitia, never from my mother or from Miss Mildred, and yet I somehow felt the latter loved me. In no letter of my father's did he ever mention Stephen Tremaine, but I read of him at times in the *Gazette*, where his name began to take a hero's measure. Proudly, too, and with tears, I often read my father's name among the foremost in honour. Excepting anxiety for him, my life at Mrs. Spencer's glided on calm and placid as a summer day. I had every instruction that the best masters could give. A French *émigré* taught me his language; another, a skilful artist, gave me lessons in drawing. I became fond of painting, and learned to limn a likeness with a rapid but correct hand. I was a wild caricaturist at the same time, and my pencil sometimes shocked Mrs. Spencer by its vagaries; yet she never saw my wildest flights, in which I indulged in the grotesque and terrible till my own fancies at times appalled and haunted me.

I look back to the first year of my stay at Mrs. Spencer's as the happiest of my life. If there was any alloy in my happiness the fault was mine. I sowed jealousy and I reaped disquiet; yet even this, though it might gnaw at times, could not always disturb the tranquil sea of my peace. To be haunted by no secrets and no terrors— to find ever a soothing voice and a caressing hand ready to help, to comfort, to encourage—to have every difficulty made plain, every effort rewarded—to be constantly thought of and tenderly cared for —this was my life. And pleasures were sprinkled on my path plentifully—joyful excursions amid the beautiful scenery, rides, drives, walks. And then our evenings——
I break off — I cannot tell of all these

things. They are gone now, gone for ever; the dear hand is cold that gave them, and I, so ungrateful then, raise streaming eyes to heaven now, and cry aloud to God for a blessing on him.

Ah! there is always something in this world amiss, and when we unriddle it let us trust that God will have mercy on our blindness and our mistakes.

## CHAPTER XVI.

I HAD been a year at Mrs. Spencer's when one day the doctor, laughing, made me come to him, and have my height measured. He had measured it the day after my arrival — not against a tree, not against a wall, but against his breast, holding his arm around me, and pressing my head there, bidding me mark the place where it rested. As he did this now, and I, half blushing, hid my face on his shoulder, I found I had to bend my head to reach it.

"And when you came here a year ago, you could creep under my arm," he said, "and the dignity of reaching my shoulder seemed an impossible ambition. Ah! I thought my pale little flower would bloom and grow in my garden."

"You have been so good and kind," I whispered, still leaning my head on his shoulder, that he might not see the tears on my cheek, for the thought of the past year's happiness swept through my heart like a reproach, so conscious was I of feelings which could bear me no fruits of peace. Oh! how many among us nourish roots of bitterness poisoning life, and then accuse their Creator or rave against fate. Surely I was

> "Vex'd with a morbid devil in my blood,
> .... And, commercing with myself,
> I lost the sense that handles daily life—
> That keeps us all in order more or less."

"Esther, my poor little birdie," said the doctor, trying to lift up my face, "what are you hiding from me now? I thought I had heard all your secrets."

"Not all," said I, clinging closer to him

to hide my confusion. Alas! I was conscious that he knew none of them. Because in our daily walks and nightly chatterings I had poured out my childish history to him—my unnatural loneliness at Treval, my wonder at seeing children at play, my grim imaginings, my terrors, and all the anguish of my yearning for affection—he fancied he knew me. And yet I had never let any note of our talk vibrate too near the caved discords within me. But how often in all this time the doctor's hand had touched the lock that shut them in, how often his voice had nearly uttered the cabalistic word that would have freed them, only I could tell. Yet I had resisted, and a year's kindness, a year's tender, watchful, love, had failed to make me show these grim skeletons to the only eye that could have exorcised them for ever.

Ah! the true reason of my silence was that I forgot them in his presence. In our evening twitterings, chirping together of twenty pleasant things, lingering by rills of laughter, and bubbling talk, flashing into wit, could I stop to hate any one?

In a land of sunshine, every view glowing in the light, my soul steeped in summer warmth, my heart, my thoughts in his hand, led by him through fresh meads and pastures ever new, while every leaf he shook down upon my head and every flower he made to spring up at my feet breathed of him, and in breathing of him sprang into comfort, life, love—while all this was so, could the hunger and emptiness of Treval come near me? could the shadow of Paul Polwhele darken my sky? could the cold Miss Mildred creep like death upon me, and touch me with her terrible secret?

No! a thousand times no!

And in all this life and light, this clear, whole, sound health he gave me—this new

way he found for my soul, bringing me out
of the wilderness into the springs of Jordan
—in this I find the secret of my silence.
I had nothing to tell when he was by me,
save that I was happy. Let me think it,
else how can I forgive myself for sealing
up my thoughts from him, and causing him
pain and sorrow? Let me reiterate to my
soul that in the full contentment of his
presence all evil died. My hate for Alice
Weston ceased to gnaw. The shadow of
Paul fled away. The thought of Miss
Mildred dwindled into quietness. Let me
tell myself again how in the evenings, when
I bounded down the stairs to meet him,
every ruffle on my spirit was smoothed, my
whole being flashed into a smile, and all I
had to tell was told in a kiss—that I was
glad, that I was one beaming joy from head
to foot—this it told him, and he was content. Thus he thought he knew me, and
I, the morbid secretiveness of whose nature

time and his hand have healed—I, who so long ago laid bare Miss Mildred's secret, and watched the shadow of Paul go down into the sea—I weep now, not for these things, but for him, and the cruel deception of that thought.

Yes, as a gardener knows a watered garden, fair and beautiful through his care, and forgets that without him it would be a waste, so Hubert Spencer knew me. He knew *his* Esther—the Esther that grew up like a flower beneath his fostering hand—the Esther of a thousand graces—all his—the Esther radiant with the charm of smile and song—all his—the Esther full of tenderness, care, watchfulness—all his—all his!

O Heaven! let me weep—let these dry and withered eyes find the relief of tears! I am old, and my brain is scorched, my heart is shrivelled—O give me tears lest I die!

See, they drop down, they find a way for themselves over wrinkled channels long arid; with a sob of thankfulness, I feel their refreshing dew softening my sorrow, and I cry in hope, "Oh, thank God, a little while and I shall see him again, in that land where all is forgiven! O Hubert! Hubert!"

Can I help it, if, breaking off in my narrative, I look back thus with yearning eyes into that past time, so clear to me, so unformed, dim, and uncertain to you, built up as it is imperfectly to your sense by my poor words?

Ah! pardon me, I am old. You must pardon much in the aged, even as we pardon much in the young. It is we, not they, who see the shadow of the lean, thin hand which will some day clutch youth, and set him face to face with a visage like his own, but wrinkled like mine—care, and sorrow, and pain, my children, stamped on it, marring its beauty. He never set out on his journey with this face, but it is his now, and we, who saw the shadow of it come on his baby brow, we are very pitiful to the young—would they were so to us!—but few are pitiful to the old, except the angels, and they know this face of pain is only a mask, which Death's hand shall take off gently, and lay down in the grave.

Was I not telling you what Hubert said to me before he went away? Before he went away! Ah, yes, my pen has reached the sore spot round which it strayed, not daring to gall it with a touch. He was going away, that is why he measured my height; that is why he looked and looked into my face as though he would have it grow into his eyes; that is why he called me "Birdie," and a thousand sweet names that fell upon my ear like a rill of music.

I cannot say I was sad when we parted;

I never could be sad while he was still with me; it was when he was gone that I —no, I did not weep, it was Jenifer who cried so bitterly, and the echo of whose sobs reached me at night when the house was still. I never wept, but I lost something of *his* Esther every day, and the old Esther grew and grew, drying up my heart, as she gained upon me step by step. It was Mr. Winterdale who took Hubert away. I had seen the letters come that disquieted him, and lastly Mr. Winterdale himself arrived, vexing our bright parlour with his cold presence, and bustling his sister into a fussy fever of delight and pride. Once during his stay, entering the room hurriedly, I overheard these words: —" There are ways in which a man can travel in spite of Bonaparte, and I tell you, Hubert, I have had sure word that the ruffian is at Munich." Then he stopped. " Good morning, Miss Treganowen. Have you slept soundly?" But not waiting for my answer, he turned again to his nephew. "I hear he is too cautious to commit any act through which he can be laid hold of, so our sole chance is bribery; such a scoundrel is surely to be bought, and he must be, for without him we have no proof——"

Here he broke off, taking the doctor to the window, and continuing the conversation in a whisper; still I was certain I heard Miss Mildred's name, and I felt sure the dearest search of Mr. Winterdale's heart was still unfulfilled.

There was an uneasiness pervading our atmosphere during his stay which affected me painfully, shutting me up in a cold silence; the same influence weighed on the doctor with its leaden dulness, shadowing the sparkling stream of his talk, and turning our sunny evenings into winter.

I observed that my sound health appeared

to annoy Mr. Winterdale. I had not before thought his hate to me so active, but it spoke out on this subject in snarling words and unkindness.

"You are grown," he said, in his hard, cold voice.

"And much improved," said his sister. "Esther is wonderfully well now.

"Too well—too well," grumbled her brother. "She is more interesting when she is ill. Get sickly and thin, Esther; I shall grow fond of you then."

I blushed scarlet, but made no attempt to answer him. The doctor came to my relief rather hotly, I fancied.

"No sickness shall ever touch Esther here," he said, "if I can help it." His tone was short and fierce, and I looked into his face surprised. "Moreover," he continued, and his eyes flashed, "it is cruel to make a child minister to so unholy a passion as revenge."

"Justice you mean," observed Mr. Winterdale, coldly. Then he kindled all of a sudden, his pale, stern face lighting up as with an inward fire. "You neglect the surest means within your power of righting your mother. Is her name and fame nothing to you? And is all your future to be sacrificed to a false sentiment of pity for a puny child?"

"Hold!" cried Dr. Spencer, hurriedly. "I owe you so much," he continued, softening his tone, "that you cannot suppose ingratitude in my case possible; but there are things I will not bear even from you. Let us discuss this matter another time. Esther, birdie"—and he put his arm around me with infinite tenderness—"shall we go nutting in the woods with Jenifer? It would be a glorious way of spending this lovely day."

"Ah, yes, do go, Hubert," said Mrs.

Spencer, kindly. "I'll put up some lunch for you in a basket."

"You are not vexed, mother, at my leaving you?" asked her son, holding out his hand to her.

I looked at the large, comely, smiling woman, and thought if she had any wrongs to redress they certainly sat very lightly on her.

We spent a merry time in the woods, and who was so happy as Jenifer when the doctor pelted her with nuts as she stood beneath the hazel-bushes to gather up the showers his busy hand flung down?

It was a merry day, long remembered, long looked back upon wistfully, every word and circumstance garnered up by memory in a golden net of love. Yet then I knew not it was the echo of the coming farewell which trembled tenderly in every tone, and vibrated even in the laughter with which the doctor made us merry. He was resolved that his last day should be a happy one, and it was.

I know now through what sad thoughts, through what uncertain clouds of grief and pain, Dr. Spencer saw his duty clearly, and fulfilled it—to me most nobly, to others painfully, but nobly too. I know now through what a weight of sorrow he struggled that day to make my last remembrance of him cheerful, sunny, tender, like himself—and he succeeded.

On my return in the evening one thing disquieted me. Mr. Winterdale had visited my sitting-room, prying into my ways and habits with curious eyes and officious touch. I knew this without asking a question. The peculiar odour of the snuff he used pervaded the apartment; and if plainer proof was wanted it was here in grains of snuff upon my books, in grains of snuff dropped on Alice Weston's dead flowers, in snuff sprinkled by flicking fingers against the pencilled list of plants—I could almost see his laughter there with it, I thought—the odious, cold, clever, curiously-searching man, how I hated him that day!

It was the morning after this that Dr. Spencer measured my height, and broke to me tenderly the fact of his departure. I have said I shed no tears; it was so utterly impossible to be sad while I could still *see* him. Sad! it was so impossible to be aught else but happy while he was by that I never thought of tears. And he fancied the parting was not very hard to the bird he had tended; he could not tell that I was but a mirror receiving the image of his brightness, his joy, his goodness, and flashing it back upon him so vivid and life-like that he took it for my own.

Alas! when his sunny presence faded out of the mirror it was cold and dead. Yet during these few lingering hours of farewell my brightness of heart never left me. As well ask the earth to be cold while summer lingers, or the sky to be dark while the sun shines. I could not be sad.

Why tell all he did for me?—all the care and thoughtfulness reaching through months and years—every moment of his time given to some watchful care for me—the kind advice, the earnest encouragement, the tender thought—I leave it all unsaid.

Then came the hurried last moments, and with an anger I could scarcely suppress, I saw large Mrs. Spencer giving to her brother the placid tears, the lingering looks, and nameless tendernesses that should have been her son's. For bony Mr. Winterdale the tears dropped slowly, decorously over her smooth cheeks, while her lips piously invoked a blessing on his wiry-haired head. Exasperated by her coldness, I lavished a warmer kindness in all my words when I spoke to Hubert Spencer; while Jenifer, I saw by her watery eyes, would have consented that minute to be metamorphosed into the roughest terrier that ever barked could she but have followed him.

"My good Jenifer," said the doctor, taking her hand kindly, "I rely on you to take care of my birdie. Remember your promise."

Jenifer tried to answer, but her speech broke into a sob, and seizing the doctor's hand, she put it to her lips without a word. He seemed to take this action as a tacit reply.

"That's right, Jenifer," he said; "you will be Esther's sure friend, I know. God bless you, my birdie! I shall be home again so soon I will not say farewell."

I was in his arms, but scarce felt his kiss upon my cheek before he was gone. I never saw Mr. Winterdale, nor heard his adieu. One figure alone filled my sight, and when that left it, darkness fell upon me and a great chill and loneliness, shivering through which I crept up-stairs silently, and, falling upon my knees, I hid my face, and shut out all things from my blank, desolate heart, save emptiness and winter.

Jenifer's distracted sobs roused me.

"Jenifer," I said, softly, lifting a white tearless face from my arm, "why are you crying? He'll be back soon."

"Never, Miss Esther; he'll never come back to this wisht house; there's no one en et cares for him. His mother never took her eyes off her brother's face; her last words, her last looks were for him. And you?—Oh! Miss Esther, how can 'ee go on so?"

"What am I doing, Jenifer?" I asked, hurriedly, as my face burned with a sudden flush.

"I don't know, Miss Esther. You seemed to me to be wrapped round about weth a shadow—a shadow hard and cold as a wall. What prison have 'ee built up for yourself,

Miss Esther, that keeps your free sperret from rushing forth to meet tha truest heart that ever beat in tha breast of man?"

I was conscious of a strange truth in these words. I felt there *was* something which held captive my free thoughts, and barred back the affection which, like a tide, would fain have swept through my soul.

"You are talking foolishly, Jenifer," I said. "Dr. Spencer never says any nonsense to me about hearts and darts like a sixpenny valentine. Moreover, I'm not quite sixteen."

"Et's my belief you're a hundred, miss," said Jenifer, sententiously, "more's tha pity. And when I said 'heart,' I didn't mean anything like valentines. Ef aal tha valentines that aal tha fools ever writ wes turned into gould they wedn't be wuth tha goodness and tha love that Dr. Spencer means to you."

Again I felt Jenifer spoke truly, yet her words vexed me, not because some instinct already told me that for some strange reason all Dr. Spencer did had reference to me and my happiness—Mr. Winterdale might not know it, but *I* knew that for me he had stayed at Clifton, for me he was gone this journey—but her words irritated me because she appeared to think my devotion in return should be boundless, and I could not make it so unless I first shattered that glittering palace in the air which my imagination had built up.

The day came when I broke that shining fabric with my own hand; but I did it then freely, not because I was expected to do it, or owed love elsewhere as a duty.

O injudicious Jenifer! it was your fault if on that day, when my prayers, and blessings, and dearest thoughts should have followed the track of *his* chariot-wheels, with their whirling dust-clouds, I turned from the long line of road, gold-sprinkled by the falling leaves of autumn, which dropped mournfully in the October wind, to gaze wistfully down into an agate and jewelled box—Miss Mildred's gift—where reposed a handful of brown dust, once a chaplet of withered leaves.

Lifting my eyes I caught my own face in a mirror, and my wistful look flashed into one of triumph. I closed the box and put my firm hand on it.

"Wait," I said, "and we shall see. Alice cannot have such a face as that."

Alas! I forgot who it was had made me beautiful.

## CHAPTER XVII.

From the first year of my stay with Mrs. Spencer I had been in the habit of receiving many little mysterious gifts, sent without name. At first I set these down to the doctor's kindness, but he denied them so earnestly that I was obliged to believe him. After his departure these gifts continued, and there was in them a wonderful divination or forestalling of my wishes, and a certain subtle, delicate comprehension of what would please, that caused me many a puzzled thought. My mother, I knew, cared too little for me to think of me thus, so after one sick hope that flashed through me with a faint warmth and then died, I gave up all idea of her being the secret donor. Yet I could fix on no other, for there were many reasons which made me reject all thought either of Miss Mildred or my father being the hidden fairy. At length, a few days after Dr. Spencer quitted us, a packet arrived for me which I fancied unravelled the mystery.

Drawings from the " Faerie Queene," exquisitely designed, and the cipher " S. T." combined with my cipher quaintly and fancifully mingled with the flowers and grotesque figures of the designs—this is what the packet contained, and I no longer doubted from whose hand the gifts came.

I did not stop to reflect that Stephen Tremaine was in the Spanish peninsula: these drawings and his initials outweighed the logic of time and distance, and I put this gift with the rest with a glowing face and a trembling hand.

Jenifer had looked upon these mysterious presents from the first with a sort of uneasy anger, which burst forth on the arrival of the last packet into a perfect flame.

"You should oughter put the rubbish in the fire, Miss Esther," she said. "You be most sixteen, and that's too ould to be having presents sent, like ould Nick sends his brimstone in disguise. There's powder and p'ison in 'em, I dessay, leastways there's imperance, which es wus. Maybe they come from thic ould fiddle-scraping daancing-maester, who looks like a shrimp upon stilts, or t'other ould pattic with the yeller and green faace, like a pumpkin turned sick, who teaches 'ee tha gibberish tha monkeys larned at tha Tower of Babil, when they tried to catch a tongue and couldn't. Maybe et's he trying to maake 'ee faal in love weth 'un."

As I only laughed, Jenifer grew more and more angry, till the sudden arrival of a letter put an instant end to our dispute.

"Marcy alive! et's from the doctor," cried

Jenifer; "do 'ee read 'un out loud, Miss Esther, do 'ee now, co."

Thus entreated, I took the letter from her hand and did as she desired.

The doctor wrote from Treval. He had seen Miss Admonitia and Miss Mildred, who was still paler and more fragile than of yore. She had asked many questions concerning me. He fancied she loved me; he might be wrong, but there was an expression on her white face when she spoke of me which had wrung his heart. He had also been to Treganowen and seen Prudence White, who sent her love to me and Jenifer. She was lonely, and wishful that her master would come back from the war and brighten the old place with his presence, but as her mistress hated the Towers so much she supposed that would never be till Miss Esther was a woman, which would be soon now. Then she asked how tall I was, and the doctor had touched his shoulder and said, "Her head comes above this," at which Prudence had laughed.

He had visited the garden, and gathered the last plum on the tree from which we had taken so many. And the fountain in the court was broken, the water gone, the basin dry and dust-choked, but the steward had promised him it should be repaired.

Tom Pengrath was quite a fine young man, but he still preferred whistling to thinking, and he still considered Miss Esther the "wonderfullest, wisest, and wishtest young lady in the 'varsal world." So the doctor had taken Tom for a servant, partly because he liked Tom's ways, and partly because it would be so pleasant to have some one with him who could talk about Esther—some one who had known her ever since, like a sea-changeling, old and sorrowful beneath the waves, but on earth called a little child of six, the tide had floated her up to Treval.

"Good Lor'!" interrupted Jenifer, "take thic timnoodle with 'un! Why, there ar'n't more brains in Tom's head than there's meat en a blown egg!"

And Tom was content, bearing a grin on his countenance which lifted his eyebrows into his hair, and sent his hair into his hat, like stubble on end. He was busy now packing the doctor's portmanteau, daintily stowing boots on the top of shirt-frills which Jenifer's clever hand had arranged into waves of crisp, curling snow.

They would embark from Falmouth tomorrow for Portsmouth; thence they should travel by coach to Dover, where they would take the packet to Ostend, from which place he would write again.

This, with a thousand kind thoughts for me meandering through the pages like a river of silver sunshine, was the doctor's letter. Stay! here was a message for Jenifer in a postscript:—

"Shake Jenifer's hand for me, Esther, my child, and tell her she lives in my mind always with your image as your friend, and every thought I waft towards England will bear something with it for her. Tell her I *rely* on her, and there is a trust in this reliance which I could not give if her heart were not pure gold, and her nature true as a bell. I am trusting my life to her, Esther, and she knows it."

I looked up, to see Jenifer's eyes streaming with tears.

"He don't ask me fur my head, do 'ee, miss?" she sobbed; "because ef he do I'll cut 'un off, and send it to 'un en a brown-paper parcel meself! Oh!" she exclaimed, warming with her subject, "two year agone I weshed to be his dog, but now it sims to me that would be poor service. I should like to be tha air he breathes, the ground he treads on, the roof that shelters him. I should like to be his greatcoat, Miss Esther, to wrap him about and keep him warm when the world was cold."

"And be hung on a peg, and forgotten all the summer, Jenifer?"

"Forgotten! and what's that, Miss Esther? Can I think sich a gentleman can be alwis remimbering me? My joy es that he should ever want my head or my hand to do his bidding—that's my joy— and not en any reward he gives, though he gives plenty. To know that I'm sometimes en his mind, 'long with you, Miss Esther, who are the apple of his eye, fills me up with thankfulness too big for words. I feel as ef a angel had carred me right up to tha sun, and dipped me en his shining light from head to foot, and steeped my heart en something warm and good that shines and shines till I'm all light."

With the doctor's letter on my lap, I listened half abstractedly, half amused.

"Poor Jenifer," said I, "I am afraid

you are very much in love with Dr. Spencer."

"In love, miss? That's a lean way of putting it. Say I ain't any longer meself, but him—his shadder, his image—a something that esn't me and esn't him, but that catches aal he es, like a glass holds and gives back your faace. Say my sperret es clean gone out of me, and hes es come en ets plaace, so that head, hand, heart only live to do his bidding."

"And what is this grand trust, Jenifer? What is it—his body being absent—that your head and hands, imbued with his spirit, are to do for him?"

"Take care of you, Miss Esther." And, to my surprise, Jenifer, clasping her hands, burst into tears. "And et's a wisht task. Oh, don't make it harder, Miss Esther, don't make me afeard to sleep by night or rest by day lest some harm should come to you. And please, miss, do 'ee burn they picturs thic old yeller pumpkin has sent."

I soothed Jenifer as well as I could, and to bribe her quietness respecting the drawings, I promised that the door between her room and mine should be left open. The night after Mr. Winterdale's departure I had found the bolt broken, and I had begged Mrs. Spencer to get it repaired, but I agreed to forego this now, as Jenifer seemed so childishly bent on it.

About this time my mother quitted Bath to reside in London, coldly writing to me that she had not time to come and wish me good-bye. She remarked that she should take a small house and try to live economically, as there was a great demand upon her money from a quarter I knew of—that person constantly writing from abroad, forcing her to send him large sums. And this was her reason for leaving Bath, as she could not alter her style of living there, where she had so many acquaintances. She would send me her address when she got to London.

This, however, she neglected to do, and for nearly two years I did not even know where she was. I bore this desertion without complaint, but it rankled in my heart and embittered it. As if, however, to compensate me for her cruel indifference, a pretty piping bullfinch was sent to me from the same unknown hand, as the initials "S. T." on the cage told me. I shed tears over the tiny songster's head. So deeply did the spirit of the gift imbue me with comfort that I felt as though the wings of some great love shadowed me about, and the yearnings of the unknown donor seeking to console me sank into my soul like the rest of a deep sleep that fills us from head to foot.

In spite of the initials, I was now somewhat shaken in my belief that I owed these gifts to Stephen Tremaine. The bird I knew came from some one that loved me—I could *feel* this, not reason on it—and Sir Stephen did not love me. Then I remembered that Miss Mildred's second name was Salome, and I began to think hers might be the secret hand that comforted me.

My father's letters came regularly, ever full of affection and alive with the incident and the stir of war; but I say nothing of these, except that fears for his safety ever kept my mind at a straining tension of anxiety.

We all know what a period of England's history this was, and though the wave of battle never broke upon our own shore, it dragged into its vortex a full tide of English life, drowning the joy of many an English home in tears of blood.

The doctor's letters were many, too, though not regular, and they had an interest for me no other letters could have, breathing as they did a solicitude more felt than spoken, and a cheerfulness, a hopefulness, and expectancy with regard to me which roused my indolent nature to exertion and bore me in triumph over many a difficulty.

Thus nearly two years slipped away, unstirred by the breath of the absent ones save as it reached us in these letters. Mr. Winterdale and Miss Admonitia were also our constant correspondents, and towards the end of this, my third year at Clifton, she began to remind me that the time was rapidly approaching when I must return to Treval. Mr. Winterdale's letters I never saw, though I remarked, with the same vague surprise, that they were read by Mrs. Spencer with more eagerness than her son's.

I have little more to relate of these two years that bears on my story, except that Jenifer practised writing indefatigably, inking herself to the elbows—often to the eyes — with such untiring industry that, soon after the doctor's departure, she could accomplish the feat of writing a letter with tolerable ease.

I mention one thing more referring to myself. Perhaps I have omitted to say that, in spite of a great natural talent for music, its drudgery oppressed and perplexed me. Urged by Dr. Spencer, I endeavoured to conquer this difficulty, my thoughts dwelling on my resolve with such intensity that a certain feverish restlessness pervaded my mind concerning it, in the midst of which I was startled to find that music too difficult for my fingers one day became suddenly easy to me the next; and so accustomed at last did I grow to this singular fact that I gained the habit of setting aside each new piece, saying, "I shall be able to play it to-morrow." Thus, with what appeared little effort, I became in these two years an accomplished musician. In other respects I think I may say

I was clever, although after the doctor left us, the same fitfulness of mood, the same silent, shut-up manner returned upon me, though in a lesser degree, that had characterized my childhood. The truth is, I was still lonely, very lonely. Jenifer was my only companion, for between Mrs. Spencer and me, in spite of her unremitting kindness, there was little real sympathy, and since her son's departure this had dwindled into mere kindliness, so I was flung back upon myself, and but for my letters I should have surely relapsed into the melancholy, morbid Esther of Treval. Lately, too, Mrs. Spencer regarded me at times with that curious look of fear which I had observed in many eyes, even Jenifer's, and several new habits began to creep into her daily mode of life which surprised me. Especially she grew nervous, and had the key of the front door brought to her every night, being particularly careful to tell me that she hid it in a different place each evening. She also locked and double-locked her own door, and examined all the windows with careful eyes. She did this so often, glancing at me, that I began tremblingly to suspect that she had heard of Paul Polwhele, and believed I should let in a gang of thieves on her in the night.

Every day she became less and less my companion, evidently regarding me with a mingled feeling of dislike and fear. I saw this, and again the old shivering loneliness, the wistful, weird feelings that had tormented me of old, returned upon me, finding my heart swept and garnished for them.

During the first year of our solitude, I hoped every month for Hubert Spencer's return, of which he spoke confidently; then he began to write with less hope, and at last, eighteen months after his departure, his letters ceased.

I grew moody and fretful under this silence, while Mrs. Spencer bore it with that placid patience peculiar to her. Large, calm, cold, she accepted this suspense with all the philosophy which substantial flesh invokes so easily to its aid. Poor Jenifer, on the contrary, grew thin and pale, her only consolation being to talk of the doctor and slumber incessantly, her grief apparently having endowed her with a singular propensity to drop asleep at all improper times and places. At length a letter from Mr. Winterdale gave us mournfully a glimpse of the truth. He had heard from a friend that his nephew was a prisoner of war, but under what circumstances, or why he was debarred from writing, we knew not.

In the shade of this new sadness I prepared to return to Treval. With what feelings, with what steady, burning determination of purpose, you who have read my history thus far can imagine.

END OF VOL. II.

LONDON:
CLAYTON AND CO., TEMPLE PRINTING WORKS,
BOUVERIE STREET, E.C.

Check Out More Titles From HardPress Classics Series In this collection we are offering thousands of classic and hard to find books. This series spans a vast array of subjects – so you are bound to find something of interest to enjoy reading and learning about.

Subjects:
Architecture
Art
Biography & Autobiography
Body, Mind &Spirit
Children & Young Adult
Dramas
Education
Fiction
History
Language Arts & Disciplines
Law
Literary Collections
Music
Poetry
Psychology
Science
…and many more.

Visit us at www.hardpress.net

# Im The Story
### personalised classic books

"Beautiful gift, lovely finish. My Niece loves it so precious!"

Helen B Brumheldon

★★★★★

**UNIQUE GIFT**

FOR KIDS, PARTNERS AND FRIENDS

## Timeless books such as:

### Kids

Alice in Wonderland · The Jungle Book · The Wonderful Wizard of Oz
Peter and Wendy · Robin Hood · The Prince and The Pauper
The Railway Children · Treasure Island · A Christmas Carol

### Adults

Romeo and Juliet · Dracula

- **Highly** Customizable
- **Change** Book's Title
- **Replace** Character's Names with yours
- **Upload** Photo for inside page
- **Add** Inscriptions

Visit **ImTheStory.com**
and order yours today!

Lightning Source UK Ltd.
Milton Keynes UK
UKHW021013010520
362627UK00022B/2731